JUST

NETWORKS

Where every byte counts...
Your path to Computer Networking

By
Moustapha Ouhmad

INTRODUCTION

Imagine a world without networks—no emails, no streaming, no online gaming, no cloud services.

Sounds impossible, right? Networks are the invisible threads that keep our digital world running. But have you ever stopped to ask: **How does it all work?**

The answer is here.

This book is your guide to understanding the concepts of networks, whether you're aiming to level up your career or just curious about what keeps the internet alive, this is the perfect place to start.

WHAT YOU'LL LEARN

- Why this book?
- What is a network?
- LAN, WAN, MAN, PAN
- Interfaces & Cables
- Networking Models
- Intro to CLI
- Ethernet Frame
- MAC Address
- ARP
- Ping
- IPv4 Addressing - Part 1
- IPv4 Addressing - Part 2
- Switch vs Hub

WHAT YOU'LL LEARN

- IPv4 Header
- Routing
- Subnetting
- VLANs
- DTP & VTP
- STP - Part 1
- STP - Part 2
- Etherchannel
- Dynamic Routing
- OSPF - Part 1
- OSPF - Part 2
- OSPF - Part 3

WHAT YOU'LL LEARN

- FHRP
- TCP & UDP
- IPv6
- ACLs
- DNS
- DHCP
- NAT
- QoS
- LAN & WAN Architectures

WHY THIS BOOK?

Networking is essential to everything we do online, but understanding it can be tricky. This book simplifies networking concepts, breaking them down into easy-to-follow explanations. Whether you're a beginner or looking to expand your skills, you'll find practical examples and clear steps to guide you.

By the end of this book, you'll have the knowledge and confidence to set up, troubleshoot, and understand networks. Networking doesn't have to be hard—this book will make it easy for you.

WHAT IS A NETWORK?

A network is just a group of computers and devices connected together to share information and resources. Imagine a network like a system of roads, where the cars are the data traveling between devices. These devices could be anything from computers, phones, and printers to servers and cameras.

When devices are connected in a network, they can share things like files, printers, and even the internet.

There are different types of networks,

but they all serve the same basic purpose: helping devices communicate with each other. Networks can be small, like the one in your home, or huge, like the internet, which is a global network that connects millions of devices around the world.

LAN, WAN, MAN, PAN

These are different types of networks, each used for connecting devices in different ways. Here's a simple breakdown:

-LAN (Local Area Network): This is the network you have at home or in a small office. It connects devices like your computer, printer, and smartphone within a small area, such as a house or building.

WAN (Wide Area Network): A WAN covers a much larger area, like a city, country, or even the entire world.

The internet is the biggest WAN, connecting millions of computers and devices all around the globe.

MAN (Metropolitan Area Network): A MAN is bigger than a LAN but smaller than a WAN. It usually covers a city or a large campus, like a university or a business district.

PAN (Personal Area Network): This is the smallest type of network, usually for connecting devices within a very short range, like your phone, smartwatch, and Bluetooth headphones. It's typically within a few meters.

INTERFACES & CABLES

ETHERNET

ethernet is not a cable, it's a collection of network protocols that work with cables such as:
- RJ-45
- CAT 5-e
- CAT 6
- CAT 7

The speed of data transportation via these cables is related to **Bits Per Second** and not **Byte Per Second.**

<u>Bit & Byte, What's the difference?</u>
0 : Bit
1 : Bit
01101001 : Byte
>> 8 Bits (Zeros And Ones) = 1 Byte

FIBER OPTICS

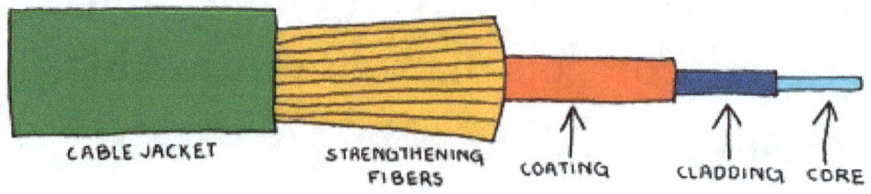

#FIBER OPTIC CABLE STRUCTURE

TYPES OF FIBER:

→ Multimode Fiber:

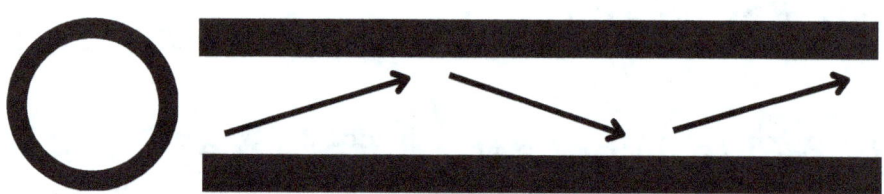

→ Singlemode Fiber:

NETWORKING MODELS

Networking models categorize and provide a structure for networking protocols

1- OSI MODEL

Sets the same network protocols structure for all types of devices to make them able to communicate with each other.

OSI Model Layers:

7-APPLICATION: 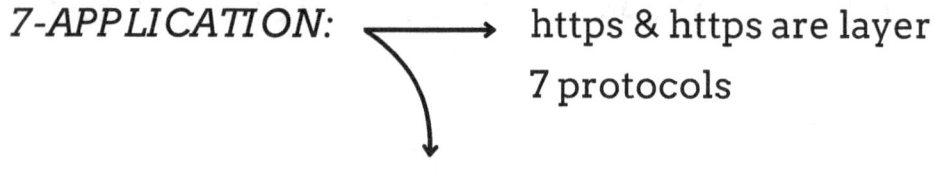 https & https are layer 7 protocols

Interact with software & apps (browser, games)

6-PRESENTATION:

Data in the *application* layer is in application format, so the presentation layer translate it to network format. (encryption of data)

5-SESSION:  Controls sessions between communicating hosts

Establishes & Manages connection between apps

4-TRANSPORT:

Breaks large pices of data into smaller segments to send it easily and prevent errors.

3- NETWORK

Provides connectivity between hosts on different networks. (Oustside _LAN_)

2- DATA LINK

It is responsible for transferring data between two devices on the same network. (inside _LAN_)

1- PHYSICAL

Defines physical characteristics used to send data (ex; voltage, physical connectors, cable specifications...)

2- TCP/IP SUITE

Similar to <u>OSI</u> but with fewer layers, it is the model used in modern networks.

TCP/IP suite Layers:

4- APPLICATION
3- TRANSPORT
2- INTERNET
1- LINK

INTRO TO CLI

Most of advanced network materials are made by CISCO. *So as a networks student you should know how to use CISCO devices such as routers and switches. For that, we will break into CLI which is very important to work with CISCO devices.*

" The operating system used in CISCO "
devices is **Cisco IOS**

CLI: Command Line Interface; The interface you use to configure cisco devices. (like Cmd in windows)

The Command Line Interface (CLI) is a way to interact with your computer using text commands instead of clicking on icons or using a mouse.

In the CLI, you type commands like "ping," "ipconfig," or "ls" to perform tasks. For example, if you want to check your IP address, you might type "ipconfig" in the CLI, and it will show you the details.

ETHERNET FRAME

ETH : Ethernet

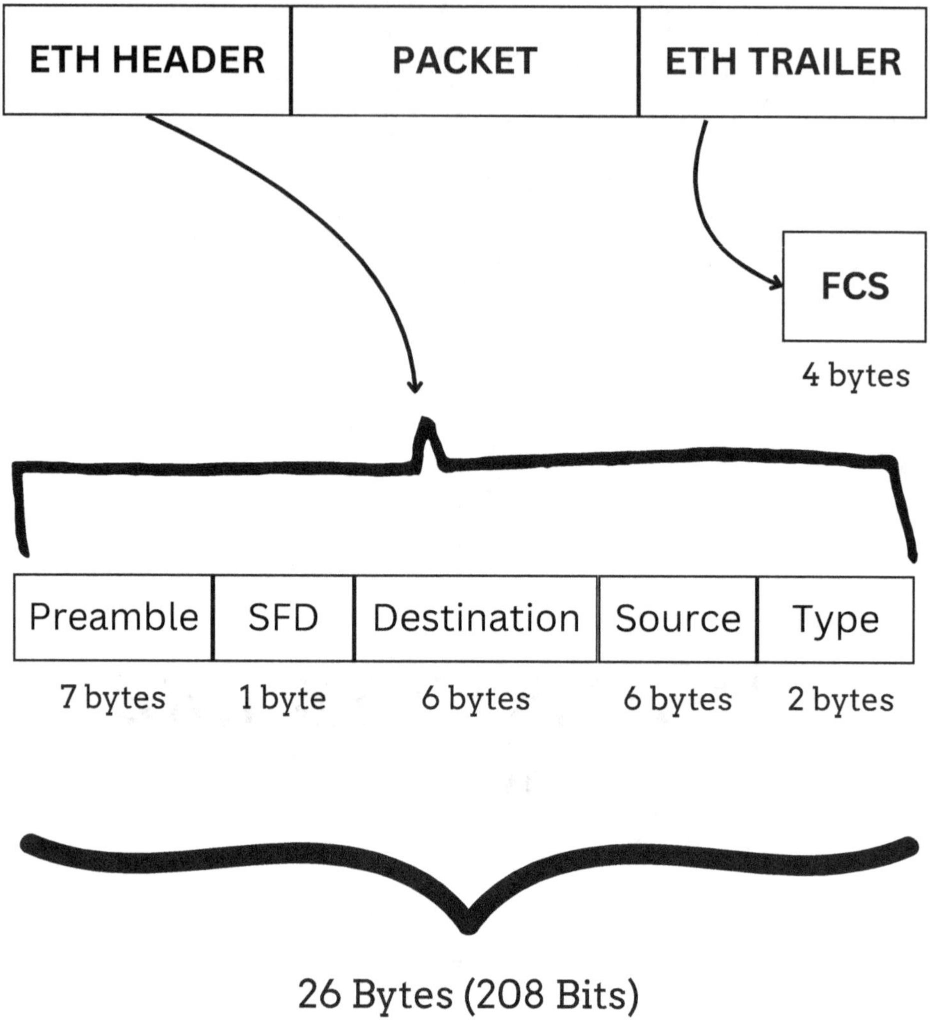

SFD: Start Frame Delimites, it's for synchronization to allow the receive option in the deviceto be prepared for receiving date.

DESTINATION: The OSI layer 2 "Address" to which the frame is being sent.

SOURCE: The OSI layer 2 "*Address*" of the device that sent the frame

TYPE: Indicates the layer 3 protocol used in encapsulated pakcet, which is almost always IPv4 or IPv6

FCS: Used by the receiving device to detect any errors that might have occured in the transmission

MAC ADDRESS

Also known as <u>*Burned-In Address BIA*</u>, it's a 6 byte physical address assigned to the device when it's made and it's globally unique.

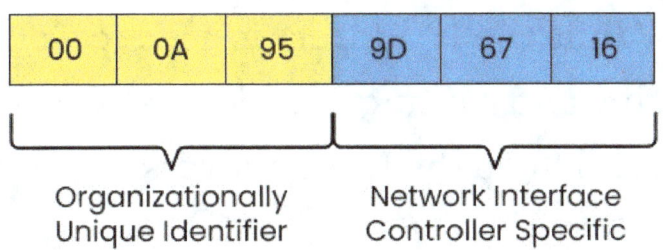

MAC ADDRESS CHARACTERISTICS:

- 6 Byte (48 bit) physical address assigned to the device when it is made.
- Globally unique for each device
- First 3 bytes are the *OUI* (Organization Unique Identifier - Not unique for the device)
- Last 3 bytes are unique to the device itself
- Written as 12 hexadecimal characters.

ARP

ARP-Address Resolution Protocol, it is used to discover the MAC address of another device that we already know its IP address.

WHY? While the IP address is used for logical addressing and routing between networks, devices still need the MAC address to communicate within the same local network. ARP resolves the IP address to a MAC address to enable direct data transmission at the hardware level within a LAN.

The ARP process consists of two messages:
- **ARP Request:** it is a message sent from the source device to all the hosts in the network, it's also know as *Flooding.*
- **ARP Reply:** Sent only to one host, which is the one who sent the ARP Request.

And when the connection is successful between the two devices, the sender saves the other device's MAC address in its *ARP Table* to reach it easily in future without sending the ARP request again and repeating the same process.

ARP Request:

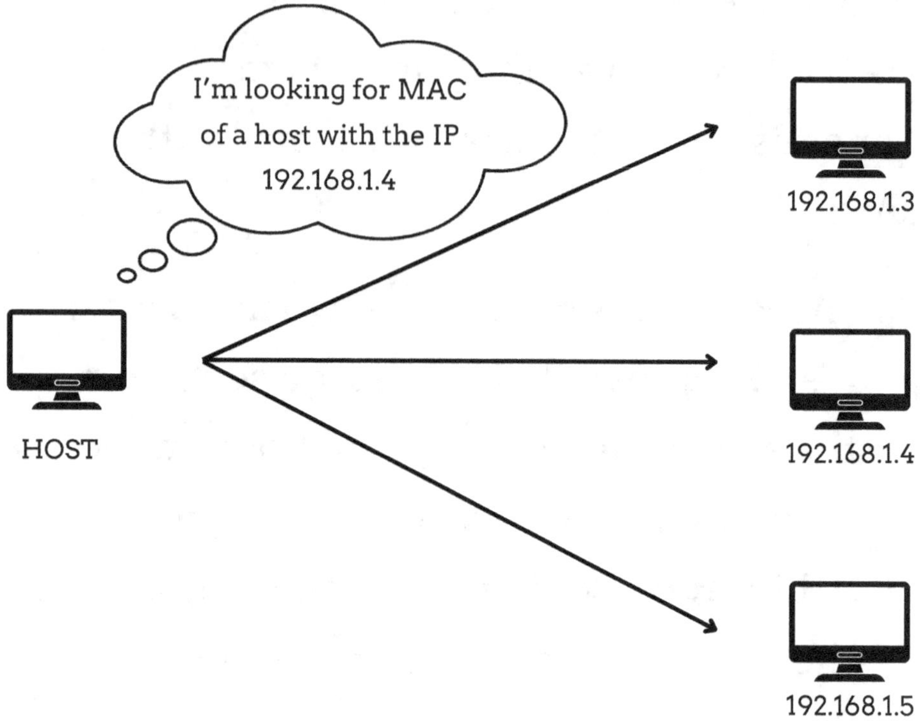

ARP Reply:

PING

Simply, Ping is a network utility that is used to test the reachability to another device. And same as MAC, it's process also consist of two messages:
- **ICMP echo request**
- **ICMP echo Reply**

But The key difference between Ping and ARP messages is that Ping sends its request directly to the target device using its IP address, whereas ARP broadcasts its request to all devices on the local network to resolve the MAC address of the target. Therefore, you cannot successfully Ping a device unless its MAC address has been obtained via an ARP request.

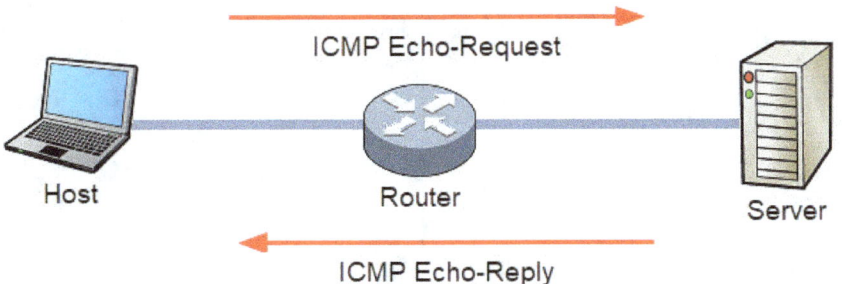

IPV4 ADDRESSING

IPv4 Addressing - Part 1

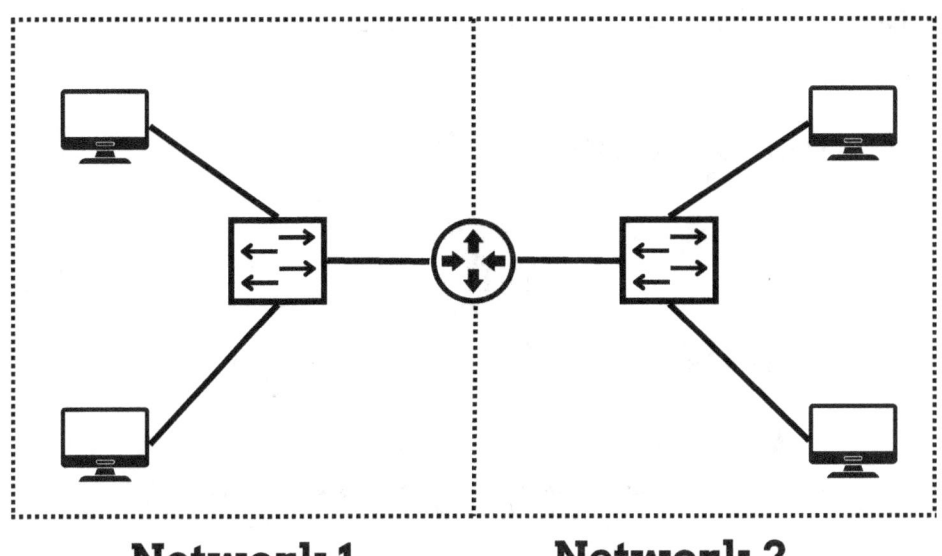

Network 1   **Network 2**

 : Router

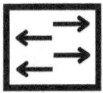 : Switch

IPv4 is the most commonly used type of IP address on the internet today. It uses a 32-bit addressing system, which allows for over 4 billion unique addresses.

This has been the standard for identifying devices on networks, although the increasing demand for IP addresses has led to the development of IPv6.

Example of an IPv4 address:

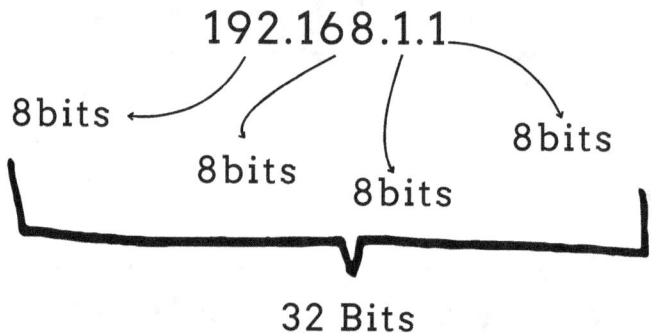

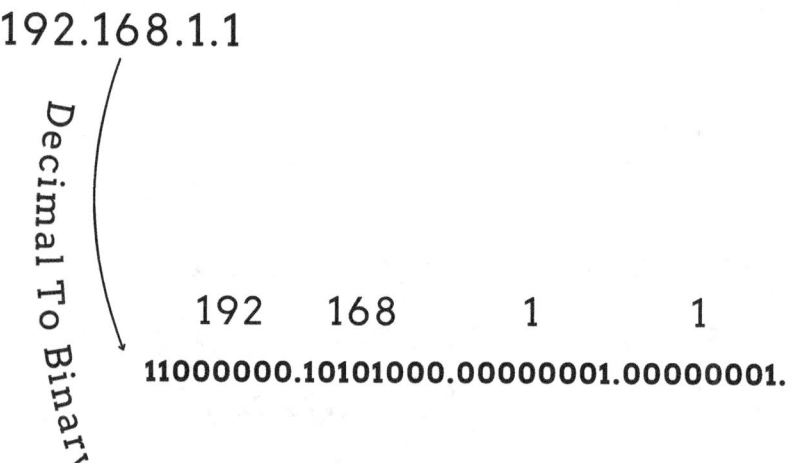

CONVERT DECIMAL TO BINARY:

To convert a decimal number to binary, follow these easy steps:

1. Start with the decimal number.
2. Divide the number by 2.
3. Write down the remainder (0 or 1).
4. Use the quotient (the result of the division) for the next step, and repeat until the quotient is 0.
5. Read the remainders backward to get the binary number.

Example: Converting 13 to binary
- $13 \div 2 = 6$, remainder 1
- $6 \div 2 = 3$, remainder 0
- $3 \div 2 = 1$, remainder 1
- $1 \div 2 = 0$, remainder 1

Now, write the remainders backwards: 1101.

So, **13 in decimal is 1101 in binary.**

Example of converting a binary IP address to decimal:

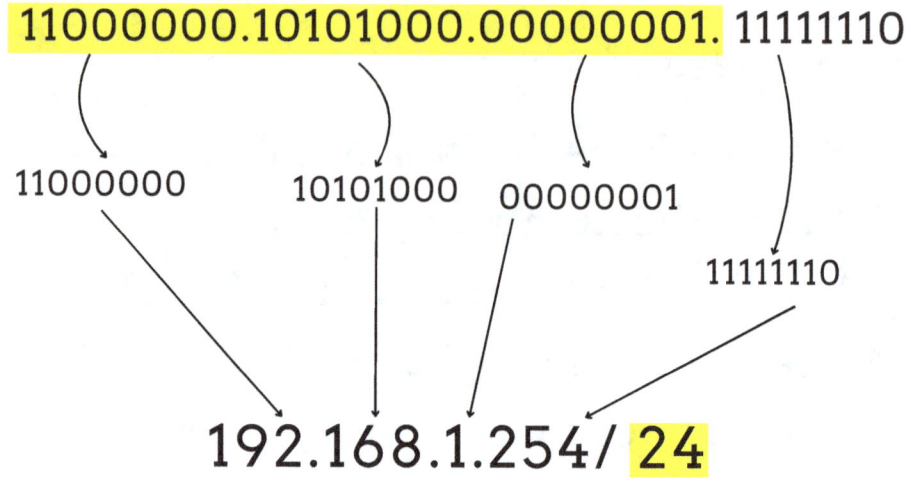

The "/24" means that the first 24 bits - *highlighted in yellow* - are reserved for the network so they don't change from device to other in the same network and it's called **NETWORK PORTION**, but the last 8 bits are speacial for each device.

note: some parts will be related to the network portion so keep this term in your mind.

IPv4 Classes:

Class	1st octet in binary	1st octet number range
A	0xxxxxxx	0-127 /8
B	10xxxxxx	128-191 /16
C	110xxxxx	192-223 /24
D	1110xxxx	224-239
E	1111xxxx	240 - 255

/8   ==> 255.0.0.0

/16 ==> 255.255.0.0

/24 ==> 255.255.255.0

IPv4 Addressing - Part 2

Maximum hosts per network:

1- Class C network

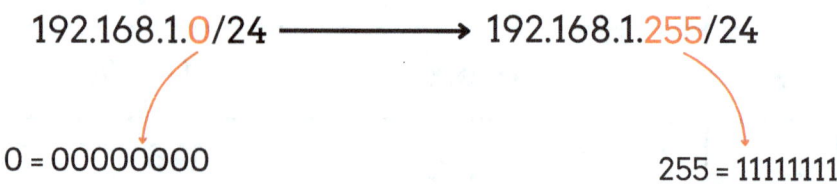

Host Portion is the number of hosts that can connect "in orange" = 8 bits => 2^8 = 256 devices in total

Maximum hosts per class C network: 2^8-2 = 254 host

2- Class B network

Host Portion "in green" = 16 bits => 2^{16} = 65536 devices in total

Maximum hosts per class B network: $2^{16}-2$ = 65534 host

3- Class A network

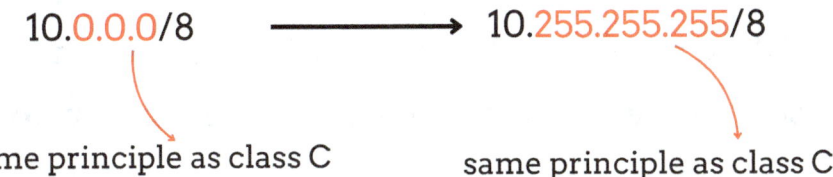

Host Portion "in red" = 24 bits => 2^24 = 16777216 devices in total

Maximum hosts per class A network: 2^24-2 = 16777214 host

<u>Summary:</u>
Maximum hosts per network => **2^n - 2**

Number of bits in the host portion

BUT WHY -2 ?

The -2 in calculating the maximum number of hosts for a subnet is because two IP addresses in each subnet are reserved and cannot be assigned to hosts:

1. <u>*Network Address:*</u>

This is the first IP address in the subnet, and it represents the subnet itself. It is used to identify the network and cannot be assigned to a device.

1. *Broadcast Address:*

This is the last IP address in the subnet, used to send messages to all devices within the subnet. It is also reserved and cannot be assigned to any host.

Size Difference Between IP Address Classes

- *Class A* networks are the largest, designed for massive networks with millions of devices.
- *Class B* networks are medium-sized, suitable for organizations with thousands of devices.
- *Class C* networks are the smallest, ideal for small networks with up to 254 devices.

SWITCH VS HUB

DUPLUEX

HALF DUPLEX: The device cannot send and receive at the same time, if it's receiving a frame it must wait before sending the next frame. commonly used in _HUB_.

FULL DUPLEX: The device can send and receive at the same time. commonly used in _SWITCH_.

SWITCH vs HUB

Hub: A hub is a simple network device that connects multiple devices in a network and broadcasts data to all connected devices, regardless of the destination. It operates at the physical layer (Layer 1) of the OSI model.

Switch: A switch is a smarter network device that connects multiple devices in a network and forwards data only to the specific device it is intended for, based on MAC addresses. It operates at the data link layer (Layer 2) of the OSI model.

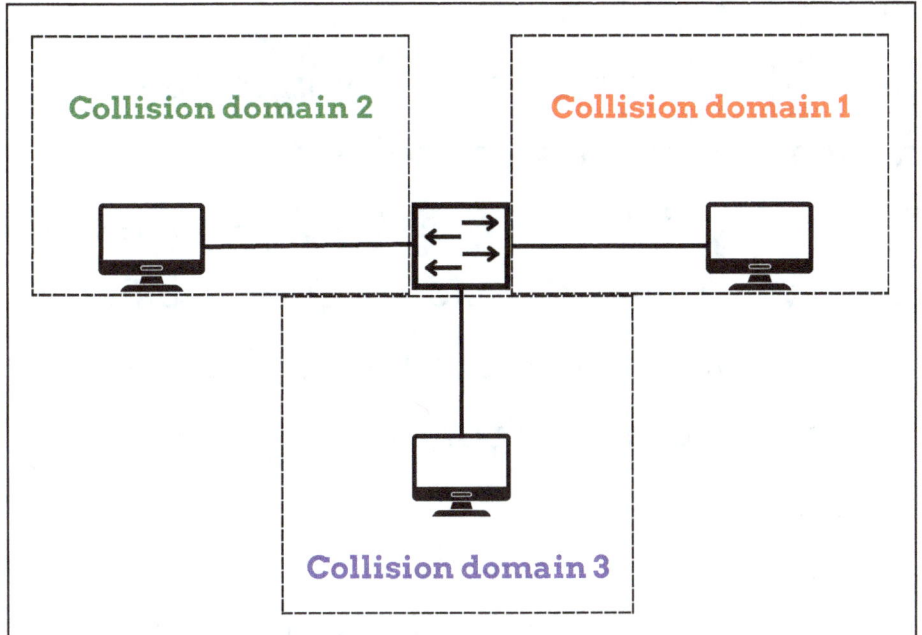

#Hosts Linked With a *Switch*

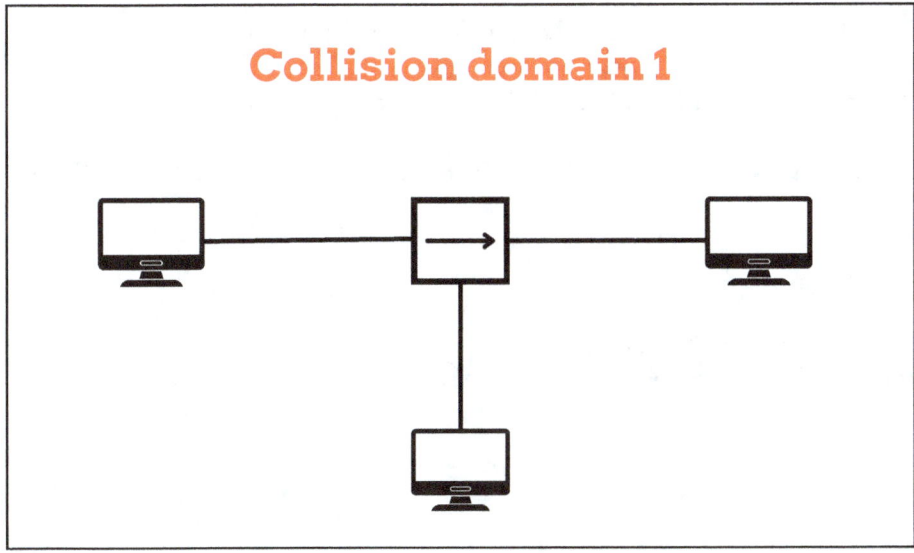

#Hosts Linked With a *HUB*

- *Hub*:

In a hub-based network, all connected devices share the same collision domain. This means if two devices try to send data at the same time, a collision occurs, causing network delays. Hubs are inefficient because the entire network is one big collision domain.

- *Switch*:

A switch creates a separate collision domain for each connected device. This means each device can communicate without interference from others, significantly reducing collisions and improving network performance.

Technical Explanation:

1. *Hub (Single Collision Domain):*
- A hub operates at the Physical Layer (Layer 1) of the OSI model and does not differentiate between devices.
- When a device sends data to the hub, the hub broadcasts the data to all connected devices. If two or more devices send data simultaneously, a collision occurs.

-Example:
- Imagine a hub connecting four devices: A, B, C, and D. If A sends data to B at the same time that C sends data to D, their signals will collide because the hub treats the entire network as a single collision domain. This collision forces all devices to stop and retransmit their data, leading to delays.

1. *Switch (Multiple Collision Domains):*
   - *A switch operates at the Data Link Layer (Layer 2) and uses MAC addresses to direct traffic.*
   - *Each port on a switch represents a separate collision domain. This means data sent by one device does not interfere with the communication of another device connected to a different port.*

-*Example:*
   - *Imagine a switch connecting the same four devices: A, B, C, and D. If A sends data to B, and at the same time C sends data to D, their communications happen independently because the switch isolates these interactions into separate collision domains. This eliminates collisions and improves efficiency.*

Conclusion:

Switches and hubs handle collision domains very differently. A hub creates a single collision domain for all connected devices, leading to frequent data collisions and network inefficiencies. In contrast, a switch provides a dedicated collision domain for each connected device, eliminating collisions and enabling faster, more reliable communication. This makes switches the preferred choice for modern networks.

IPV4 HEADER

Octet		0							1								2								3							
Octet	Bit	0	1	2	3	4	5	6	7	8	9	10	11	12	13	14	15	16	17	18	19	20	21	22	23	24	25	26	27	28	29	30	31
0		Version				IHL				DSCP						ECN		TOTAL LENGTH															
4		Identification																Flags			fragment offset												
8		Time To Live TTL								Protocol								Header Checksum															
12		Source IP address																															
16		Destination IP address																															
20		Options																															

Not included in header
{ DATA }

- *Version:*

it identifies the version of the IP (IPv4 or IPv6)

- *IHL (internet header length):*

indicates the size of the header in 32-bit words. It tells where the data (payload) starts. The minimum value is 5 (20 bytes), and it increases if options are included.

- *DSCP*:

Used to prioritize and classify network traffic for quality of service (QoS). It helps ensure that important data, like video calls or streaming, gets faster and more reliable delivery.

- *ECN:*

Provides End-to-End notification of network congestion without dropping packets.

- *Total Length:*

Indicates the entire size of the IP packet, including both the header and the data.

- *Identification*:

is used to uniquely identify a fragmented IP packet. When a large packet is broken into smaller fragments for transmission, the Identification field helps the receiving device reassemble the fragments into the original packet. Each fragment of the same original packet carries the same Identification value.

- *flags:*

Used to control and identify fragments.

- *Fragment offset:*

specifies the position (or offset) of a fragment relative to the beginning of the original packet. It helps reassemble fragmented packets in the correct order.

- *Time To Live TTL:*

Each time the packet passes through a router, the TTL is decreased by 1. When TTL reaches 0, the packet is dropped.

- *Protocol:*

Indicates the protocol of the encapsulated layer 4 PDU.

\>> Value of 6 : TCP   ;   Value of 17 : UDP
\>> Value of 1 : ICMP   ;   Value of 81 : OSPF

- *Header Checksum:*

used for error-checking the integrity of the header. It helps detect any corruption or errors that might have occurred in the header during transmission. The checksum is calculated by the sender and verified by the receiver. If the checksum doesn't match, the packet is discarded. Note that the checksum only covers the header, not the entire packet.

- *Options:*

allows additional control or configuration information to be included in the packet. This can include settings like timestamping, security features, or routing instructions.

ROUTING

Routing is the process that routers use to determine the path that IP packets should take over a network to reach their destination by storing routes to all of their known destinations in a *routing table.*

How do routers identify and determine possible routes?

There are two methods:

Dynamic Routing and *Static routing.*

Static Routing

Static routing is a method where network routes are manually configured by a network administrator. These routes do not change unless the administrator updates them. It is simple but lacks flexibility, as it doesn't adapt to network changes automatically.

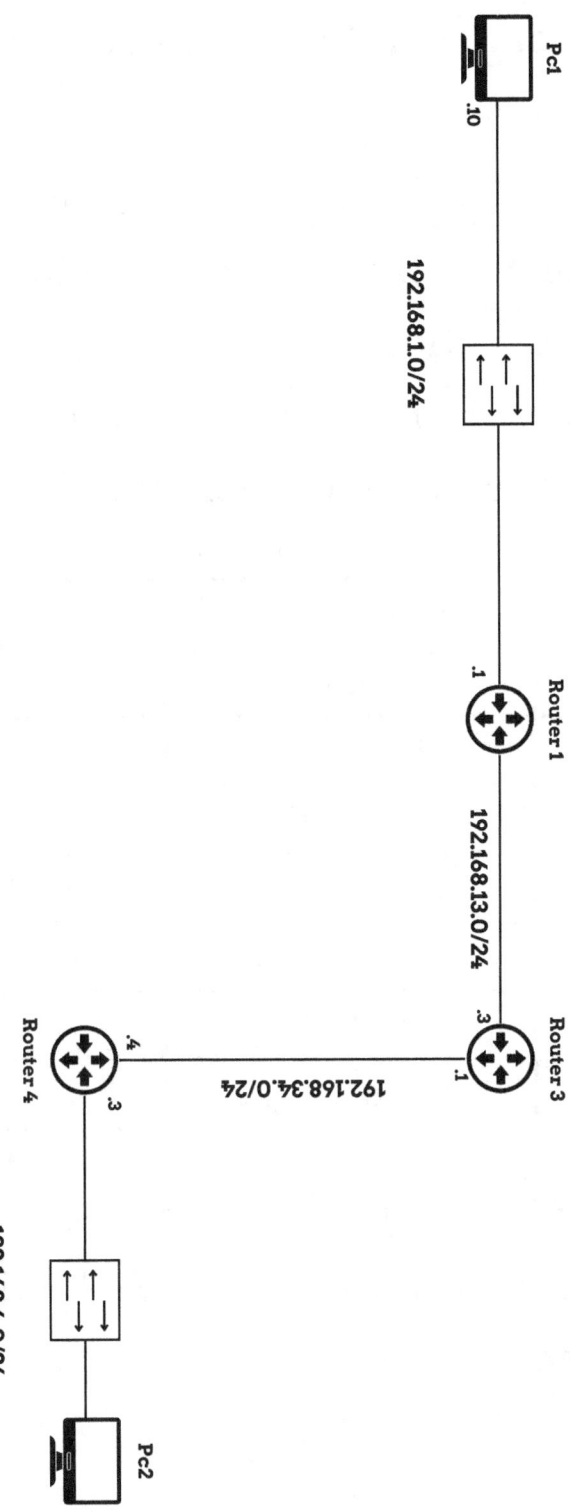

How to connect Pc1 and Pc2 even if routes are different?

Simply, the packet is sent to the default gateway which is the router to create a route to the destination.

The table below shows the routing table needed if Pc1 want to reach Pc2.

Router	Source	Next Hop
	Destination	
1	192.168.1.0/24	Connected
	192.168.4.0/24	192.168.13.3
3	192.168.1.0/24	192.168.13.1
	192.168.4.0/24	192.168.34.4
4	192.168.1.0/24	192.168.34.3
	192.168.4.0/24	Connected

After configuring each router with the configuration above, Pc1 and Pc2 will be able to connect to each other.

How to connect Pc1 and Pc2 even if routes are different?

Simply, the packet is sent to the default gateway which is the router to create a route to the destination.

The table below shows the routing table needed if Pc1 want to reach Pc2.

Router	Source	Next Hop
	Destination	
1	192.168.1.0/24	Connected
	192.168.4.0/24	192.168.13.3
3	192.168.1.0/24	192.168.13.1
	192.168.4.0/24	192.168.34.4
4	192.168.1.0/24	192.168.34.3
	192.168.4.0/24	Connected

After configuring each router with the configuration above, Pc1 and Pc2 will be able to connect to each other.

Conslusion:

Static Routing is a method where routes are manually set by a network administrator. In static routing, the administrator defines the next hop—the next router or gateway to which the packet should be sent to reach its destination. These routes remain fixed and do not change unless manually updated. It's simple but doesn't adjust automatically to network changes.

SUBNETTING

IP addresses of companies are assigned by IANA - a non profit organization

#Internet_Assigned_Numbers_Authority

Example:

-> A very large company might receive a class A or B network.

-> A small company might receive a class C network.

But, this system causes a *waste of IP addresses.*

Real example of IP waste:

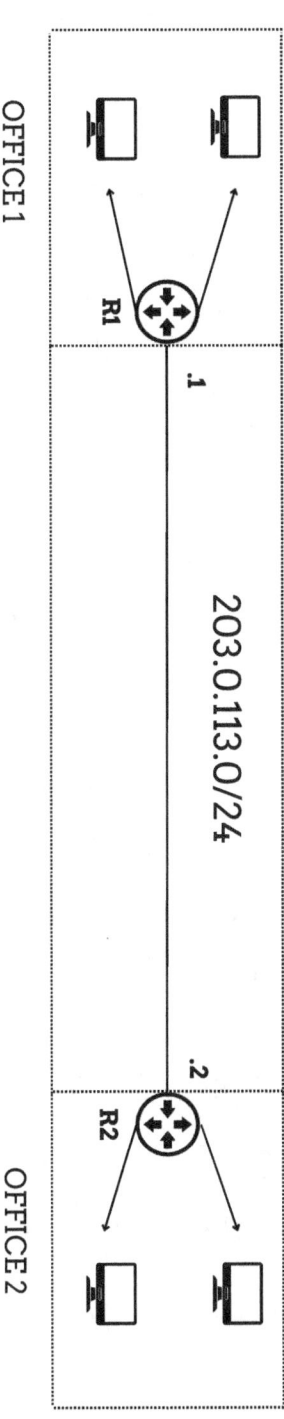

Proof Of Waste:
- -1 IP Network Address(203.0.113.0)
- -1 Broadcast addresses
- -R1 address
- -R2 address

TOTAL: only 4 IP addresses are used

While this network is C network so it has 256 IP addresses available for use but it uses only 4 IPs, then: 256IP - 4IP = 252 wasted "not used" IP addreses

CIDR

The IP addresses wasting will affect the connectivity to internet in future while there only 4 billion IP addresses in the worl.
For that, in 1993 the CIDR was introduced to replace the calssful addressing system.

CIDR (Classless Inter-Domain Routing) was introduced to remove the rigid rules of classful addressing, such as:
- Class A = /8
- Class B = /16
- Class C = /24

This allowed larger network to be split into smaller networks called *"Subnets - Subnetworks"*

HOW THIS WORKS?

The CIDR allows to use different prefixe lengths, so it doesn't base only on /24 for example

Prefix Length: /8 , /16 . /24 ...etc

With CIDR, the following IP address

203.0.113.0/24

Can be:

203.0.113.0/25
203.0.113.0/26
203.0.113.0/27
203.0.113.0/28
203.0.113.0/29
203.0.113.0/30

This will expand the "Netowrk Portion" and reduce the number of hosts.
Example:
Number of hosts in 203.0.113.0/25 is
2^7-2=126 IP
So using /25 instead of /24 reduced it from 254 IP to 126 IP and we saved 128 IP

Note: The example above is only for class C networks, so in other classes it can be /17 , /18 , /19 ... etc. But, the process and the concept are the same for all the classes.

Real-life example:

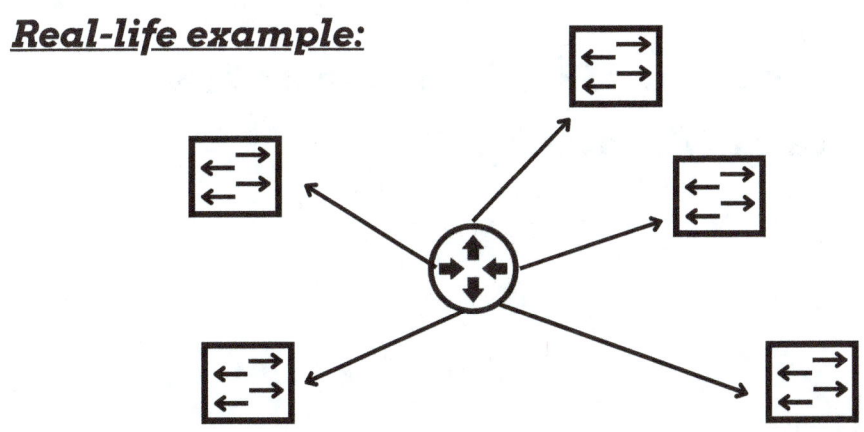

In this network with the IP **192.168.255.0** we have 5 subnets. And to know the appropriate subnetmask we use this formula:

2^x = Number of subnets in need

with X : number of borrowed "added" bits.

So in this example we have 2^3 is the appropriate one.

Why? Because:

>> 2^1 = 2 and its smaller than 5 which is the number of hosts

>> 2^2 = 4 and it is also smaller than 5 so it's not enough

>> **2^3 = 8** and 8>5 , so it is enough for this network because we are able to connect 8 devices while we need to connect only 5 devices.

How the binary IP will look from /24 network to /28 network?

A /24 Netowrk:

24 bits are reserved for the network which is called network portion

A /28 Netowrk:

24 bits are reserved for the network which is called network portion

The hosts portion "in green" became smaller from /24 to /28, that's how we reduce the used IPs and prevent IP wasting

Prefix Length	Number of subnets	Number of hosts
/25	2	126
/26	4	62
/27	8	30
/28	16	14
/29	32	6
/30	64	2

The explanation is for class C network, but it is the same process and concept for other classes.

Important note:
All what we did before is called **FLSM** - Fixed length subnet mask.
Now, let's explore **VLSM** which is more useful.

CIDR - VLSM

allows you to divide an IP address range into subnets of different sizes based on the specific needs of each network. Unlike FLSM, where all subnets must have the same size, VLSM is more efficient because it minimizes wasted IP addresses.

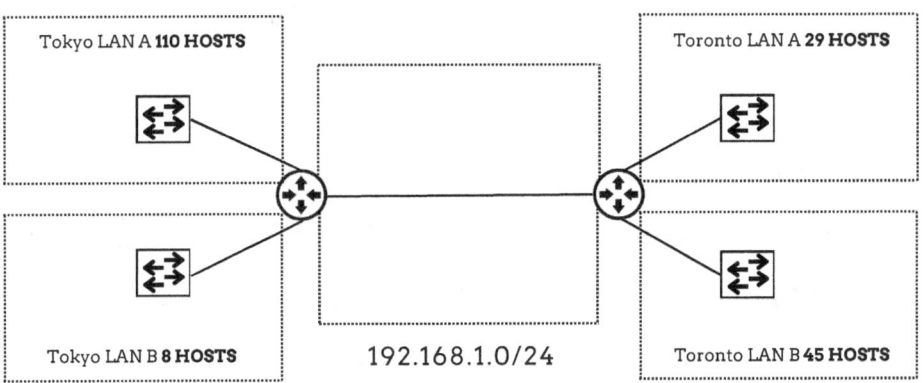

If we use FLSM and divide the IP into 5 subnets, borrowing 3 bits will leave 5 host bits (8 - 3 = 5). This gives 2^5=32 total addresses per subnet, with 30 usable IPs. This is not enough for Tokyo LAN A (110 hosts) or Toronto LAN B (45 hosts).

For that, we will subnet this network using VLSM, and to do that we should start with the order from the Largest network to the lowest network.

Order
1- Tokyo LAN A   : **192.168.1.0/25**
2- Toronto LAN B : **192.168.1.0/26**
3- Toronto LAN A : **192.168.1.0/27**
4- Tokyo LAN B   : **192.168.1.0/28**

AS we said before, in VLSM each subnet have a specific *Prefix Length*, unlike FLSM where all the subnets ue the same Prefix Length.

Conclusion:

VLSM (Variable Length Subnet Mask) allows for more efficient IP address utilization by enabling subnets of different sizes, tailored to the specific needs of each network. Unlike FLSM, where all subnets have the same size, VLSM offers flexibility by allocating just the right number of IPs to each subnet. This reduces waste and maximizes address space, making it ideal for networks with varying requirements. Proper planning is essential to avoid overlap and ensure optimal use of available IP addresses.

VLANS

VLAN - PART 1

is a logical grouping of devices within a network, regardless of their physical location. It allows network administrators to segment a larger network into smaller, isolated networks for improved security, performance, and management. Devices within the same VLAN can communicate directly, while communication between different VLANs typically requires a router or Layer 3 switch.

Broadcast Domain:
is a group of devices that will receive a broadcast frame sent by any other device within the same network segment.

Why using VLAN and how it helps?

VLANs (Virtual Local Area Networks) provide several benefits to network design and management:

- **Improved Security:** By segmenting a network into smaller, isolated VLANs, you can limit the spread of broadcast traffic and ensure sensitive data is confined to specific groups, reducing the risk of unauthorized access.

- **Better Performance:** VLANs reduce broadcast traffic by containing broadcasts within the VLAN. This minimizes unnecessary traffic on other parts of the network, improving overall performance.
- **Simplified Network Management:** VLANs make it easier to manage large networks by logically grouping devices based on their function (e.g., HR, Sales, IT) rather than physical location. This simplifies network administration and configuration.
- **Flexibility and Scalability:** VLANs allow for easier changes to network structure without needing to re-cable. Devices in different physical locations can be grouped into the same VLAN, providing flexibility as the network grows.
- **Network Segmentation:** VLANs enable the segmentation of a network into different broadcast domains, which helps in better traffic management and reducing network congestion.

In summary, VLANs enhance security, performance, and network efficiency by isolating traffic, reducing congestion, and simplifying network management.

Real-Life example:

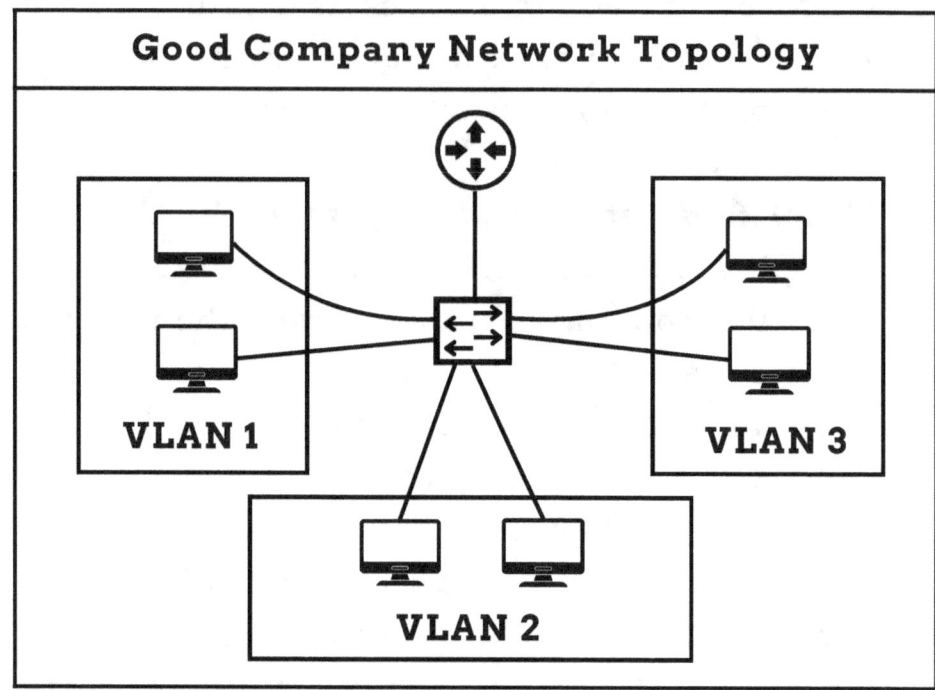

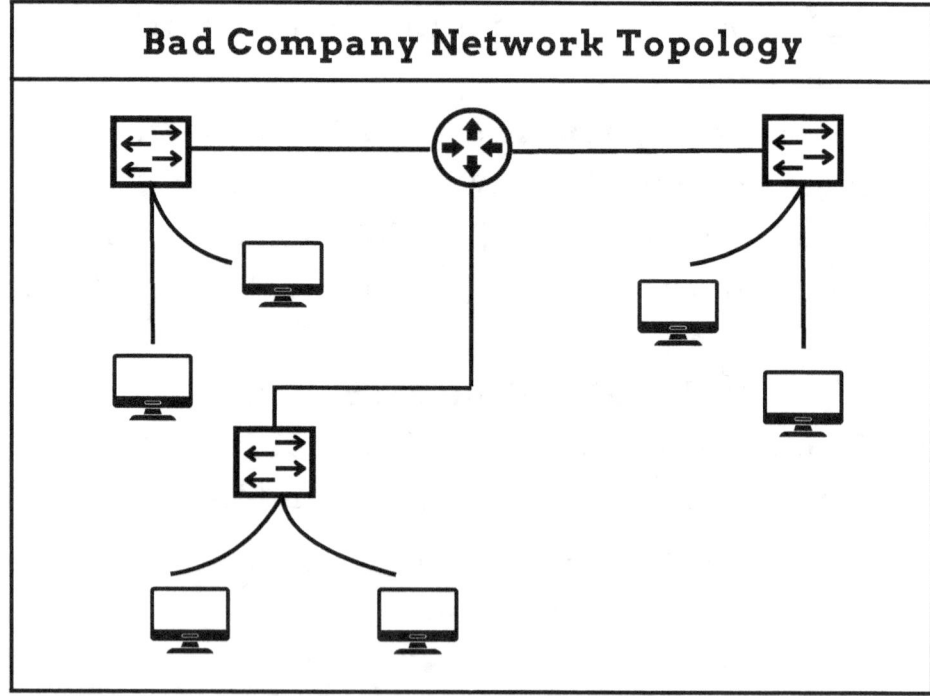

"In the previous example, we saw that in the optimal topology, we separated each department into a single VLAN, resulting in 4 VLANs in total. Now, if two PCs from different VLANs want to communicate, the switch will not simply flood the message. Instead, it will require a router or Layer 3 switch -*in this case we use layer 3 switch*- to route the traffic between the VLANs."

This clarification emphasizes that communication between different VLANs requires routing, which is typically done by a router or a Layer 3 switch.

What is flooding:

refers to the process of sending a data packet to all devices in a network or a segment, rather than a specific destination. This typically happens when a network device, like a switch or router, doesn't have a known path or forwarding rule for a particular destination address.

VLAN - PART 2

VLAN TAGGING:
is a method used to identify and separate traffic from different VLANs on a network. It involves adding a special tag to the Ethernet frame, known as the VLAN tag, which contains the VLAN ID (identifier). This allows network devices like switches to recognize which VLAN the frame belongs to and properly forward it to the correct destination, even when multiple VLANs share the same physical network link. VLAN tagging is commonly used in **802.1Q** standard, which enables trunking between switches, allowing multiple VLANs to traverse a single physical link.

802.1 TAG FROMAT

16 BITS	3 BITS	1 BIT	12 BITS
PID	TCI		
	PCP	DEI	VID

PID: Always set to value of 0x8100 which indicates that the frame is 802.1Q tagged.
PCP: Used for Class of Service (CoS)
DEI: Used to indicate the frame that can be dropped if the network is congested.
VID: Vlan Id, it identifies the VLAN thatthe frame blongs to.

Note: When a switch receives an *untagged* frame on a trunk port,, it assumes the frame to the *Native Vlan* which is VLAN1 by default on all trunk ports.

Router on a Stick (ROAS)
is a network configuration where a single router is used to route traffic between multiple VLANs. The router has one physical interface connected to a trunk link, which carries traffic for multiple VLANs. The router uses subinterfaces, each assigned to a different VLAN, to route the traffic between them.

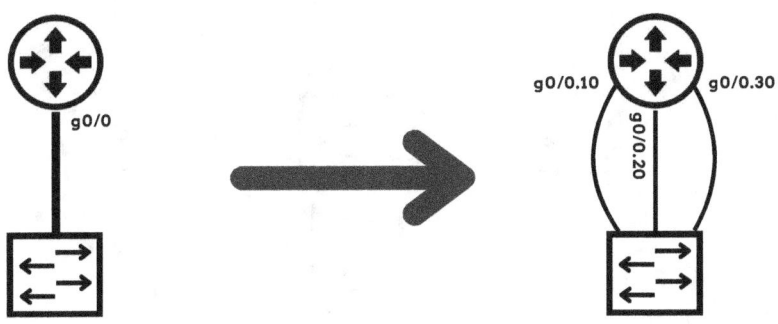

SVI	

SVI (Switched Virtual Interface):
is a virtual interface on a switch that allows the switch to perform Layer 3 routing for VLANs. It acts as the gateway for devices within a specific VLAN, enabling inter-VLAN communication. An SVI is typically configured on a Layer 3 switch, where each VLAN is assigned a unique IP address, and the switch can route traffic between different VLANs.

We configure each PC to use the SVI as their gateway address instead of the router so all the traffic will be sent and routed by the switch.

EXAMPLE:

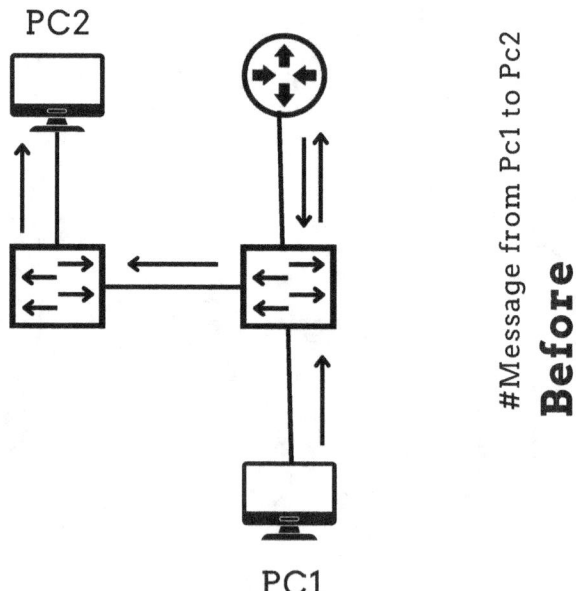

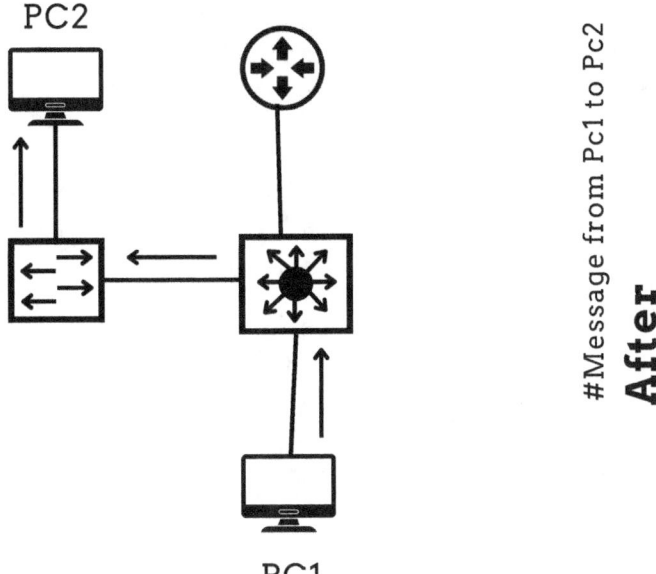

 **Layer 3 switch**

is a network device that combines the functionality of a traditional Layer 2 switch and a router. It can perform switching within VLANs (Layer 2) and routing between VLANs (Layer 3) without needing an external router. This makes it ideal for managing traffic in larger networks with multiple VLANs, offering high-speed performance and efficient inter-VLAN communication.

DTP & VTP

DTP

DTP is a cisco protocol that allows Cisco switches to dynamically dertermine their interface status if it's either Trunk or Access.

Access Port: A switch port configured to carry traffic for a single VLAN. It connects end devices like PCs or printers to the network.
Trunk Port: A switch port that carries traffic for multiple VLANs, allowing them to share a single connection between switches.

A switch in dynamic desirable mode will actively form a Trunk if it's connected to another switch port in the following modes:
- Trunk mode
- Dynamic desirable mode
- dynamic auto mode

Dynamic Desirable Mode: The switch actively tries to negotiate and form a trunk link with the connected device.
Dynamic Auto Mode: The switch passively waits for the other device to initiate trunk negotiation.

Administrative Mode	Trunk	Dynamic Desirable	Access	Dynamic Auto
Trunk	Trunk	Trunk	✕	Trunk
Dynamic Desirable	Trunk	Trunk	Access	Trunk
Access	✕	Access	Access	Access
Dynamic Auto	Trunk	Trunk	Access	Access

DTP

DTP is a cisco protocol that allows Cisco switches to dynamically dertermine their interface status if it's either Trunk or Access.

Access Port: A switch port configured to carry traffic for a single VLAN. It connects end devices like PCs or printers to the network.
Trunk Port: A switch port that carries traffic for multiple VLANs, allowing them to share a single connection between switches.

A switch in dynamic desirable mode will actively form a Trunk if it's connected to another switch port in the following modes:
- Trunk mode
- Dynamic desirable mode
- dynamic auto mode

Dynamic Desirable Mode: The switch actively tries to negotiate and form a trunk link with the connected device.
Dynamic Auto Mode: The switch passively waits for the other device to initiate trunk negotiation.

VTP

VTP (VLAN Trunking Protocol) is a Cisco protocol that helps switches automatically share and manage VLAN information like VLAN IDs, names, and configurations across a network. It reduces the need for manual setup by synchronizing VLAN details between switches connected through trunk links.
It allows you to configure VLANs on a central VTP server switch, and other switches (clients) will synchronize their VLAN database to the VTP server.

It's designed for large networks with many VLANs, so that there is no need to configure each VLAN on every switch.

VTP modes: Server, Client or Transparent:

-> server:
- Can modify, add, delete VLANs
- Stores vlan database in Non-volatile RAM
- It also functions as a Client.

-> Client:
- Can't modify or delete
- doesn't store database in Non-volatile RAM\

-> Transparent:
- Doesn't participate in the VTP domain (doesn't synchronize its VLAN database)

VTP Summary:
- VTP allows you to configure VLANs on a central VTP server switch
- it's designed for large networks
- it's rarely used and not recommended
- it has 3 versions: VTPv1, VTPv2, VTPv3
- Cisco switches operate in VTP server mode by default

STP

STP - PART 1 & 2

#Network redundancy:

Networks today should work 24/7/365, so a cut-off may cause a lot of problems to the business and the network design is a factor that can affect positively or negatively.

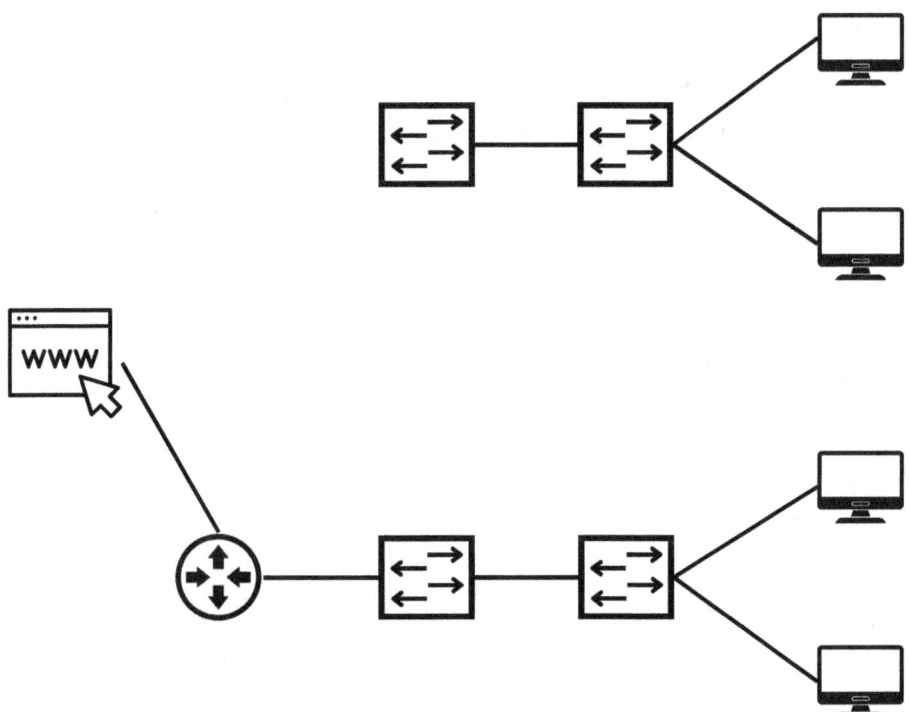

#BAD NETWORK TOPOLOGY:

If a problem occures between router & internet, all the network will shut=down

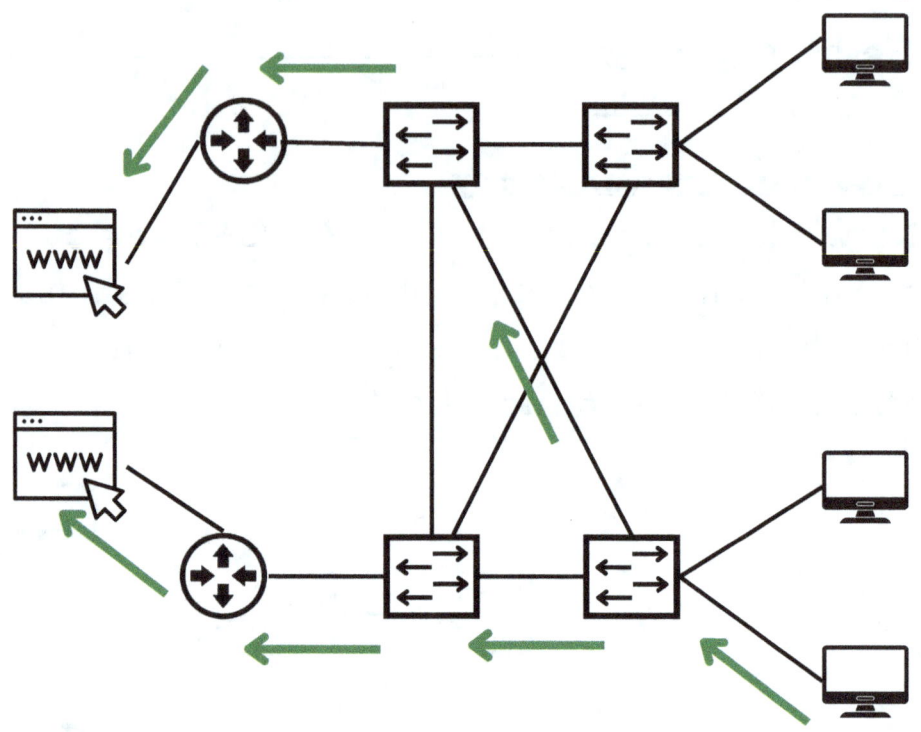

#GOOD NETWORK TOPOLOGY:

Pcs have more available ways to reach the Internet.

#Broadcast Storm:

Infinite loop of flooding data
->Problem: Mac Address Flapping; when frames with the same source MAC repeatdly arrive, the switch keep updating its MAC table continuously.
So *STP* was invented to solve this problem by selecting ports that will forward data and port that will block data instead of forwarding it, all that to avoid loops.

Example:

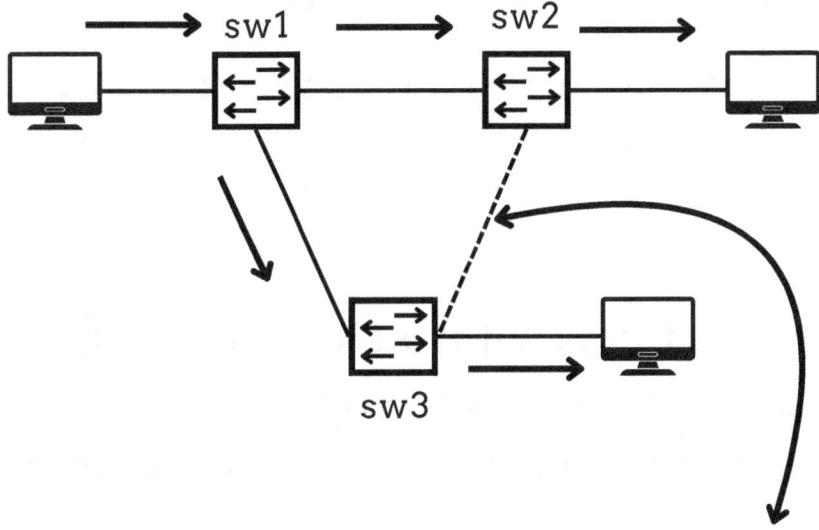

This connection is set as **blocking** to avoid Loop of Flooding between sw2 and sw3, and this is done by STP

#Bridge ID:

Bridge ID	
Bridge Priority 16 bits	**Mac Address** 48 bits

Switch with lowest *bridge priority* becomes Root Bridge. But, if bridge priority is equal on all switches, then the switch with lowest Mac address becomes root bridge.

If switch port connected to a device, the port is set to forwarding but if it's connected to a switch then it's set to blocking. Only Root Bridge have all ports set to forwarding.

Each remaining switch select one of its interfaces to be its **root port.** the interface with *lowest* Cost wil be the root port.

Interface Cost.

Interface Speed	STP Cost
10 mbps	100
100 mbps	19
1 Gbps	4
10 Gbps	2

if two ports have the same cost, then the port connected to the lowest neighbor bridge ID will be the Root Port

#State of Port.

STP port state	Stable/transitional
Blocking	Stable
Listening	Transitional
Learning	Transitional
Forwarding	Stable

- **Blocking**: The port doesn't forward traffic or learn MAC addresses. It only listens for BPDU messages to prevent loops.
- **Listening**: The port prepares to transition by listening to BPDU messages but still doesn't forward traffic or learn MAC addresses.

- **Learning**: The port begins learning MAC addresses but still doesn't forward traffic.
- **Forwarding**: The port actively forwards traffic and continues learning MAC addresses, fully participating in the network.

What is BPDU?

is a network message used by switches in the Spanning Tree Protocol (STP) to exchange information about topology and prevent network loops.

#STP Port state properties:

STP port state	Frame forwarding	MAC learning
Blocking	NO	NO
Listening	NO	NO
Learning	NO	Yes
Forwarding	Yes	Yes
Disabling	NO	NO

BPDU Guard:

is a security feature on switches that prevents unauthorized BPDUs from being received on a port. If a BPDU is detected on a port configured with BPDU Guard, the port is immediately put into a disabled state to protect the network from potential topology changes or loops.

ETHERCHANNEL

Etherchannel is a technology that allows multiple physical links to be combined into a single logical link, acting as one interface to increase bandwidth and provide redundancy. It can be used on both Layer 2 (switching) and Layer 3 (routing) interfaces.

#Without Etherchannel:

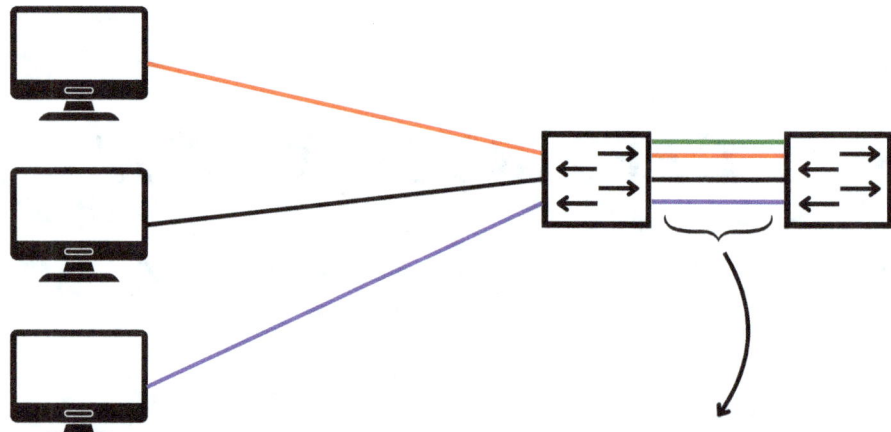

These 4 cables will never increase speed because **STP** blocks 3 of them to avoid layer 2 loops.

#With Etherchannel:

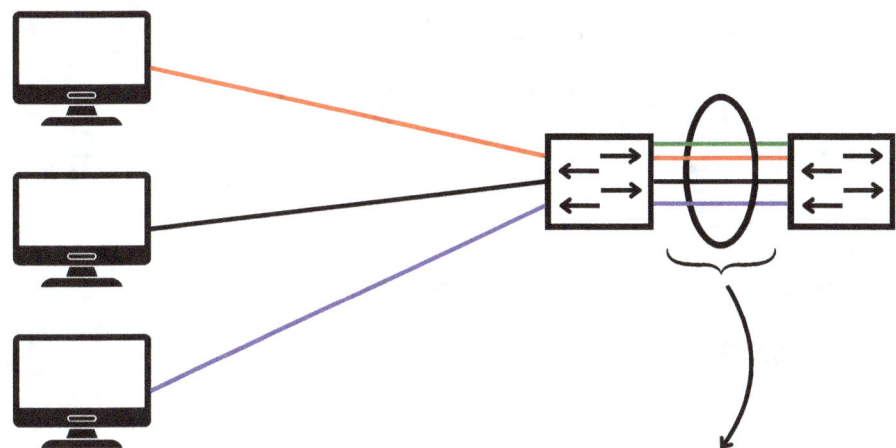

The circle means that all those interfaces will act as a single interface and STP will not block anyone of them so the speed will increase

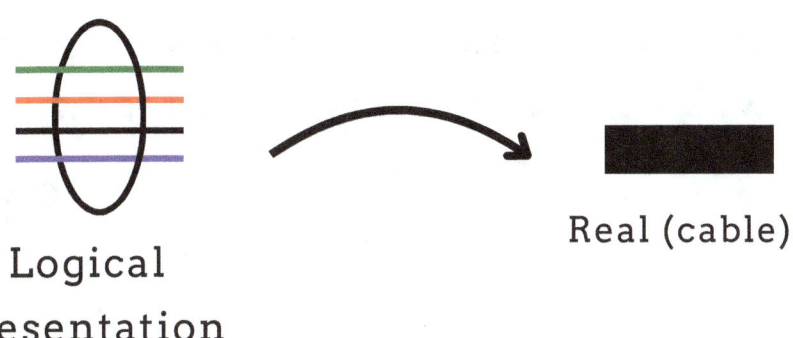

Logical presentation

Real (cable)

-PAgP (Port Aggregation Protocol)

-> It's works only in Cisco devices
-> Dynamically negotiate the creation/maintenance of Etherchannel.

-LACP (Link Aggregation Control Protocol)

-> is an IEEE 802.1AX standard protocol used to combine multiple physical network links into a single logical link, known as an EtherChannel. LACP helps manage the aggregation by allowing devices to automatically detect and configure the links, ensuring redundancy and increased bandwidth. It is vendor-neutral and works on devices from different manufacturers.

DYNAMIC ROUTING

Dynamic Routing is a method used by routers to automatically adjust and find the best path for data to travel across a network. Unlike static routing, where routes are manually configured, dynamic routing protocols allow routers to exchange information and make real-time decisions about the most efficient routes based on network conditions.

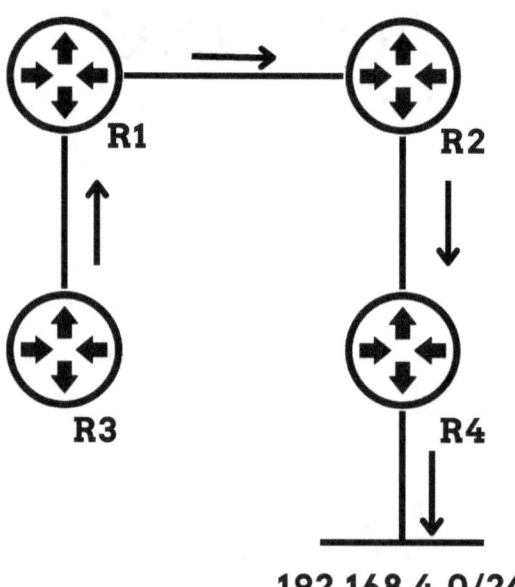

if those routers are configured to dynamic routing and R4 isn't working, then R1 will automatically remove R4 from its table.

Dynamic Routing Protocols:

-> **IGP:** Used to share routes within a single Autonomous System (AS) which means a single organization

-> **EGP:** Used to share routes between multiple organizations

Example:

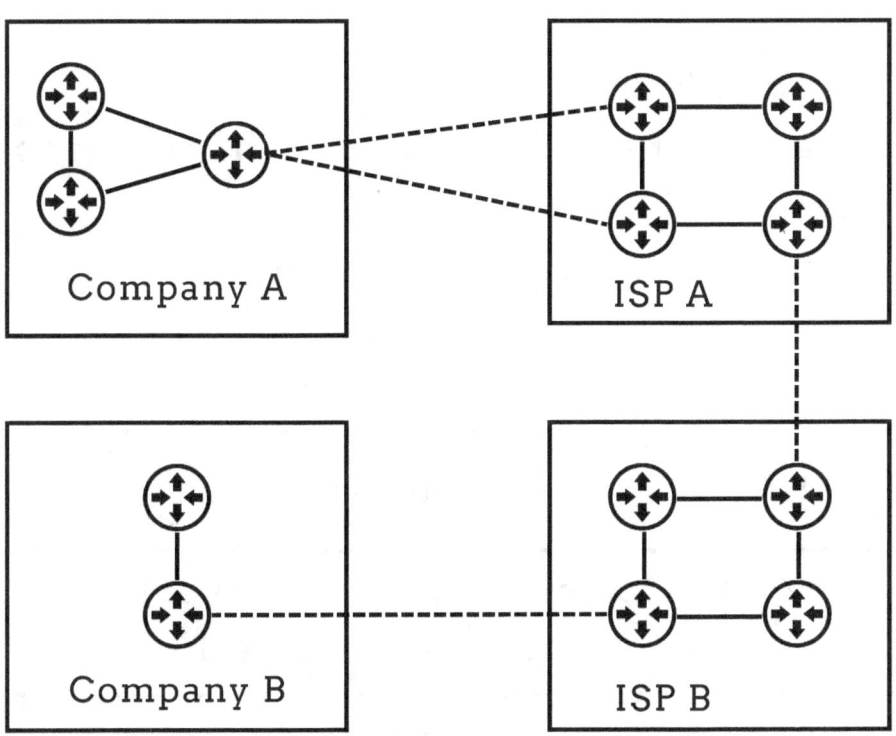

ISP: Internet Service Provider

| : IGP   ; | EGP

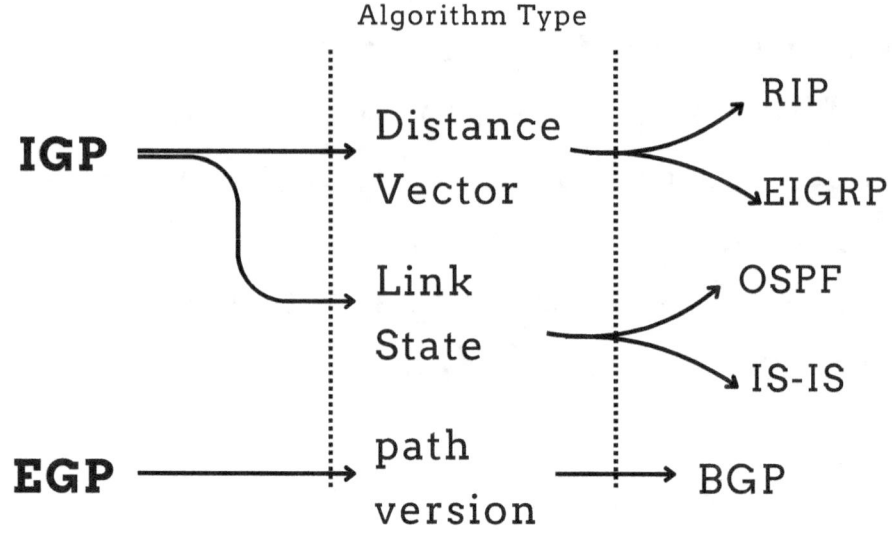

Metric Value:

Router use the Metric Value of the routes to determine the best route.

-> Lower Metric value = best route

IGP	Metric
RIP	Hop Count
EIGRP	Metric based on bandwidth and delay by default
OSPF	Cost
IS-IS	Cost

Administrative Distance (AD):

Used to determine which routing protocol is better.

-> Lower AD = better to use.

Route	AD
eBGP	20
EIGRP	90
IGRP	100
OSPF	110
IS-IS	115
RIP	120
iBGP	200
Unusable route	255

OSPF

OSPF - PART1

OSPF (Open Shortest Path First) is a dynamic routing protocol used to find the best path for data within a network. It works by dividing the network into areas and using the *Dijkstra* algorithm (Shortest Path First) to calculate the shortest path. OSPF is efficient, supports large networks, and quickly adapts to changes in network topology.

OSPF versions:
OSPFv1 (1989): Not used anymore
OSPFv2 (1998): Used in IPv4
OSPFv3 (2008): Used in IPv6

Link State protocol:
-> When using link state, each router creates a connectivity map of the network, to allow this, each router advertises information about its interfaces to its neighbors. Routers use this map to calculate the best route.

is OSPF a link state protocol? YES

-Routers store information about the network in **LSAs** (Link State Advertisements), which are organized in a structure called **LSDB** (Link State Database). Then, routers _flood LSAs_ until all routers in the OSPF area develop the same map of the network.

LSA Flooding

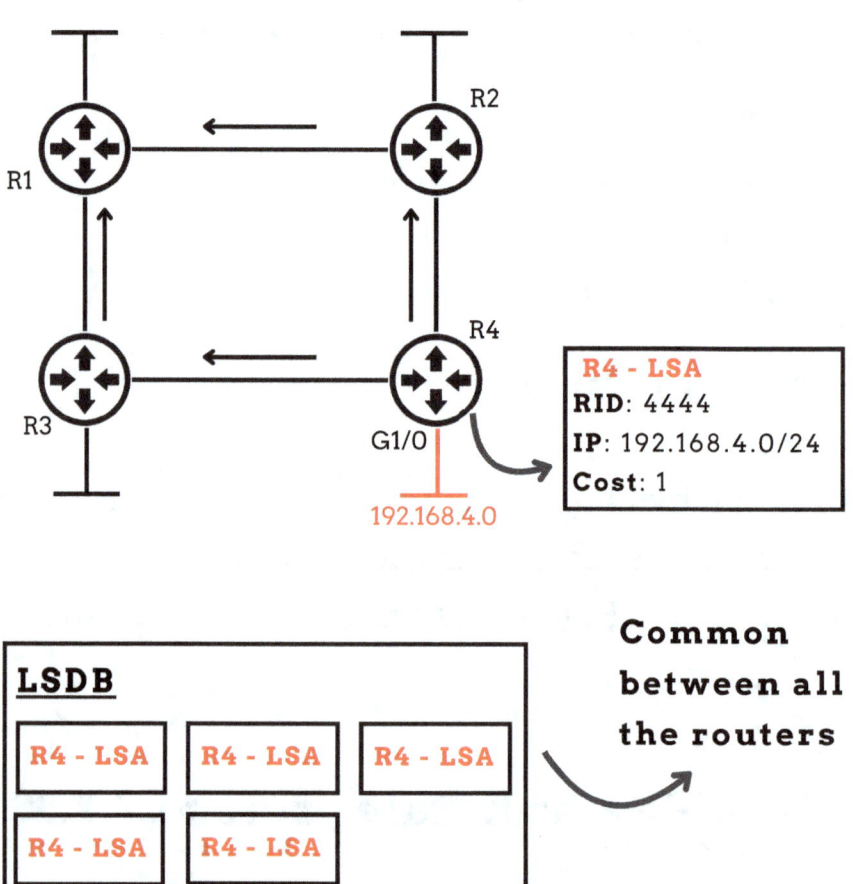

Common between all the routers

Explanation:

- OSPF is enabled on R4's G1/0 interface
- R4 creates an LSA (R4 - LSA) to tell its neighbors about the network in G1/0 "192.168.4.0"
- The LAS is flooded through the network until all other routers receive it
- After receiving, now all routers share the same _LSDB_
- Then, each route uses the SPF algorithm to calculate the best route to reach the network 192.168.4.0

Steps of sharing LSAs:

1- Become neighbors with other router is the same area

2- Exchange LSAs

3- Calculate the best route.

OSPF Area:

An area is a set of routers and links that share the same **LSDB**.

-> **Area 0 (Backbone):** is the most important area that all other areas must connect to.

-> Routers with all interfaces in same area are called *Internal Routers*.

-> Routers with interfaces in multiple areas are called *ABRs*

-> **Intra-area Route:** Destination inside the same OSPF area.

-> **Interarea Route:** destinaton in different OSPF area

OSPF RULES

- OSPF areas mustn't be split
- All OSPF areas must have an *ABR* connected to *backbone* area

Example:

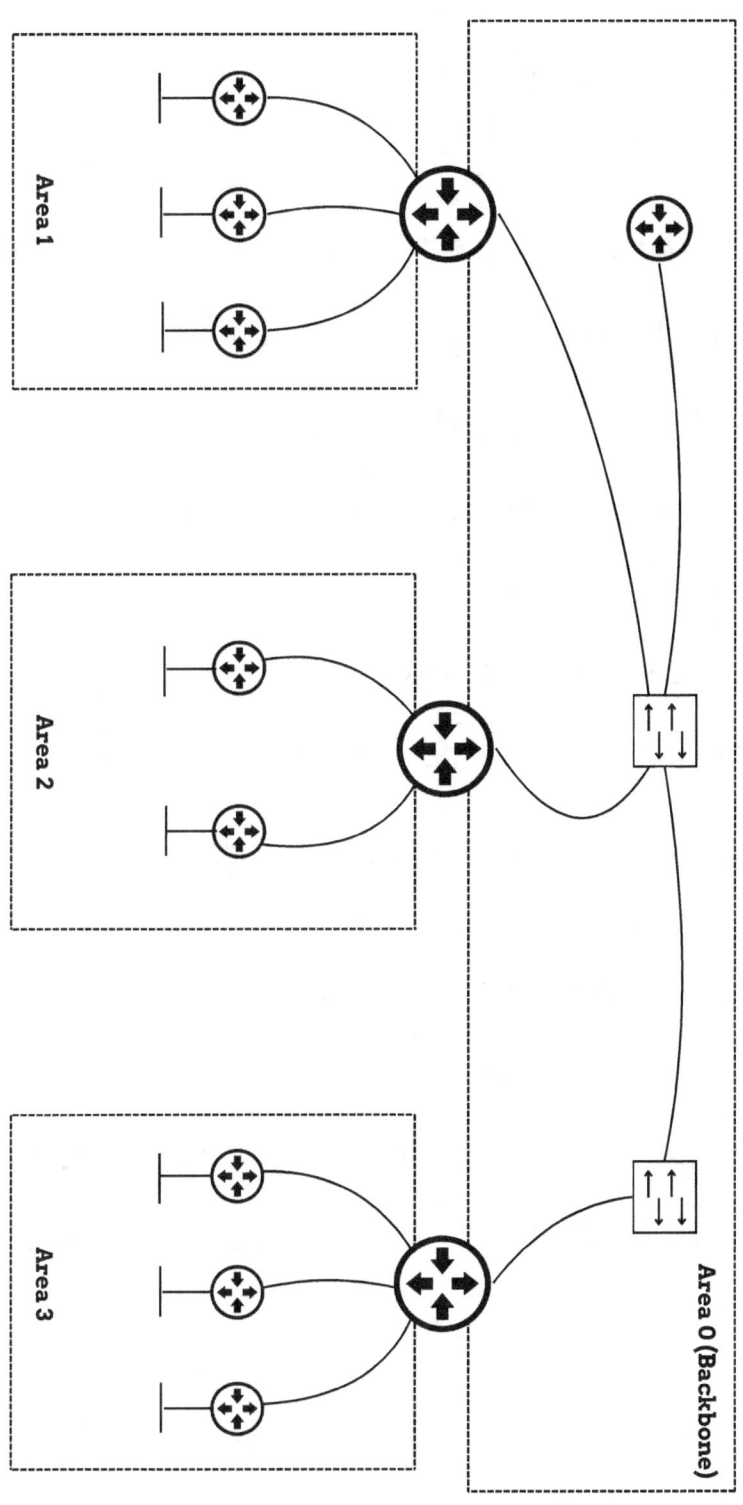

OSPF - PART 2

OSPF Metric -> **Cost** (Calculated based on the bandwidth of the interface).

How the cost is calculated?

It's calculated by dividing a reference bandwidth value by the interface's bandwidth.

$$\frac{\text{Reference bandwidth}}{\text{Interface's bandwidth}} = \text{Cost}$$

The default reference bandwidth is *100mbps*
Note: All OSPF routers should have the same refrence bandwidth.

OSPF Neighbors

- Routers cannot do the work of sharing network info, calculating routes...etc, <u>if they are not neighbors</u>

"Neighboring" Steps:

Steps that OSPF routers go through to form a neighbor relationship and share the same Link State Database (LSDB).

1. Down State
- The initial state where no OSPF packets have been sent or received.
- The router waits to discover neighbors.

2. Init State
- A router sends a Hello packet to discover neighbors.
- It includes information like its Router ID, subnet mask, timers, and area ID.
- At this point, the router is waiting for a response from potential neighbors.

3. Two-Way State
- The router receives a Hello packet from a neighbor that lists its own Router ID.
- If the Router ID is recognized in the received Hello packet, the neighbor relationship is established.

4. ExStart State
- Neighbors decide which router will act as the Master and the Slave for database synchronization.
- The Master sends a Database Description (DBD) packet first, and the Slave responds to it.

5. Exchange State
- Routers exchange DBD packets, which contain summaries of their LSDBs.
- The purpose is to determine which LSAs are missing or outdated.

6. Loading State
- The router requests missing or outdated LSAs from its neighbor using Link State Request (LSR) packets.
- The neighbor responds with Link State Update (LSU) packets, containing the requested LSAs.

7. Full State
- The routers' LSDBs are now fully synchronized.
- They transition to the Full State, meaning the neighbor relationship is fully formed.

Steps Summary:

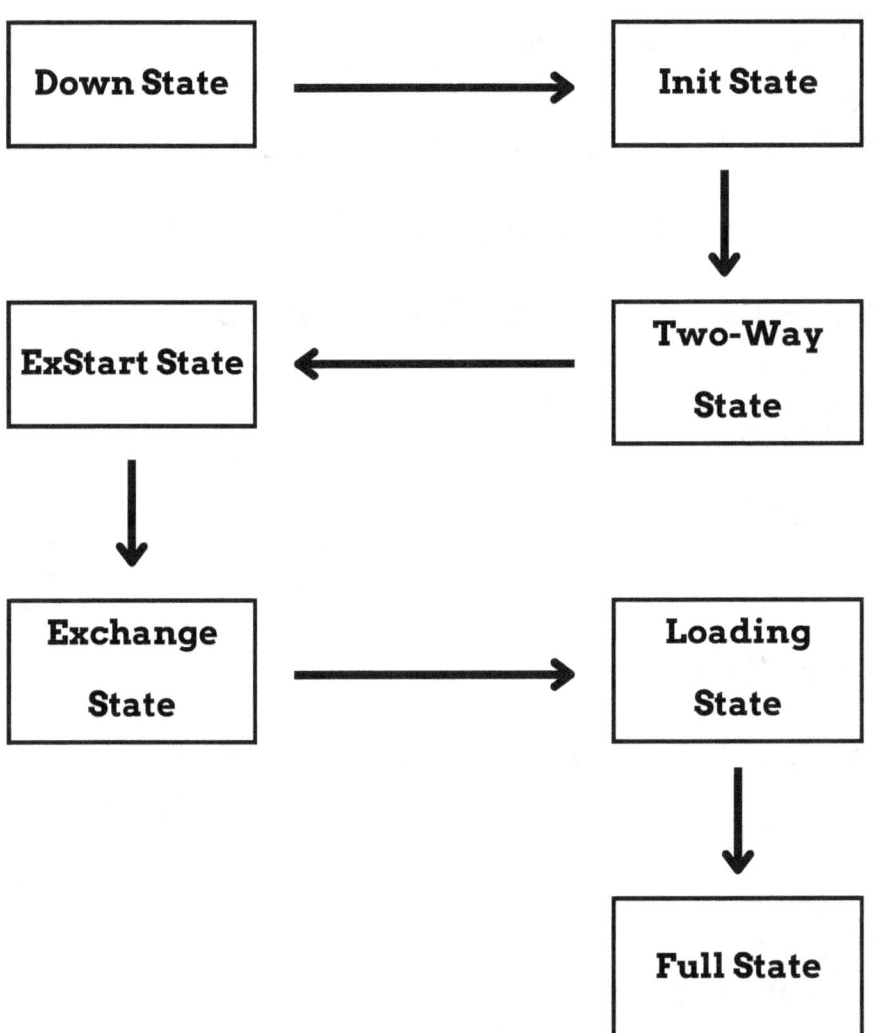

OSPF - PART 3

OSPF Networks Type

OSPF network type refers to the type of communication between <u>OSPF neighbors.</u> There are 3 main OSPF network types:

-Broadcast:

Enabled by default on ethernet interfaces

-Point To Point:

Enabled by default on Point to Point and HDLC interfaces.

-Non Broadcast:

Enabled by default on Frame Relay and X.25 interfaces.

Broadcast

It's a method of communication where a message is sent from one device to all devices on the same network segment.

In OSPF broadcast networks, routers dynamically discover neighbors.

-A **DR** (Designated Router) and **BDR** (Backup Designated Router) must be elected on each subnet.

Designated Router (DR): In OSPF, the DR is the main router chosen in a network to share and manage routing information, making communication more efficient.

Backup Designated Router (BDR): The BDR is a backup router that takes over if the DR stops working.

Point To Point

-Enabled on <u>serial interfaces</u> using PPP or HDLC encapsulations.

-Routers dynamically discover neighbors.

-Unlike broadcast networks, a DR and BDR are not elected because point-to-point connections only have two devices, so there is no need for a DR or BDR."

Serial Interfaces:

- <u>DCE</u> (Data Circuit-Terminating Equipment): Provides the clocking signal to control the data flow, typically used on the provider's side.
- <u>DTE</u> (Data Terminal Equipment): Receives the clocking signal, usually the router or device on the user's side.

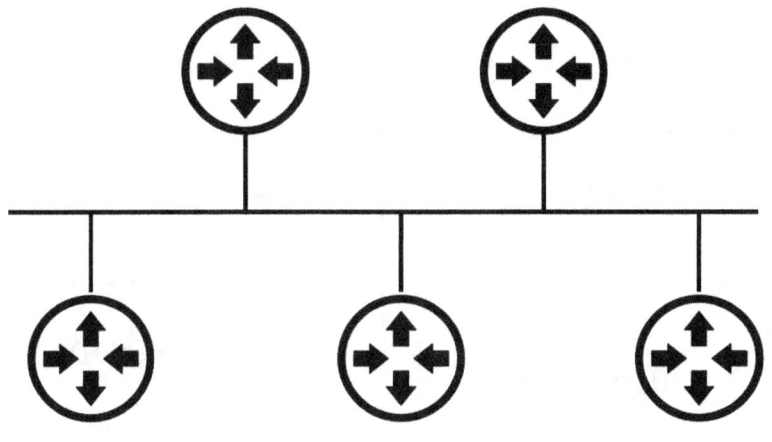

 # Broadcast #

 # Point to Point #

OSPF Neighbor Requirements:

1- Areas must match

2- Interfaces must be at the same subnet

3- OSPF RIDs must be unique

4- Hello and Dead time must match

5- IP MTU settings must match

6- OSPF network type must match

Summary:

Broadcast	Point To Point
Default on Ethernet	Default on HDLC and PPP
DR and DBR are elected	No DR / DBR
Neighbors dynamically discovered	Same as Broadcast
Default timers: Hello:10 Dead:40	Same as Broadcast

FHRP

FHRP (First Hop Redundancy Protocol) FHRP is not a single protocol, it's a group of protocols that ensure network availability by automatically switching to a backup gateway if the main one fails. This keeps devices connected without interruption.

example:

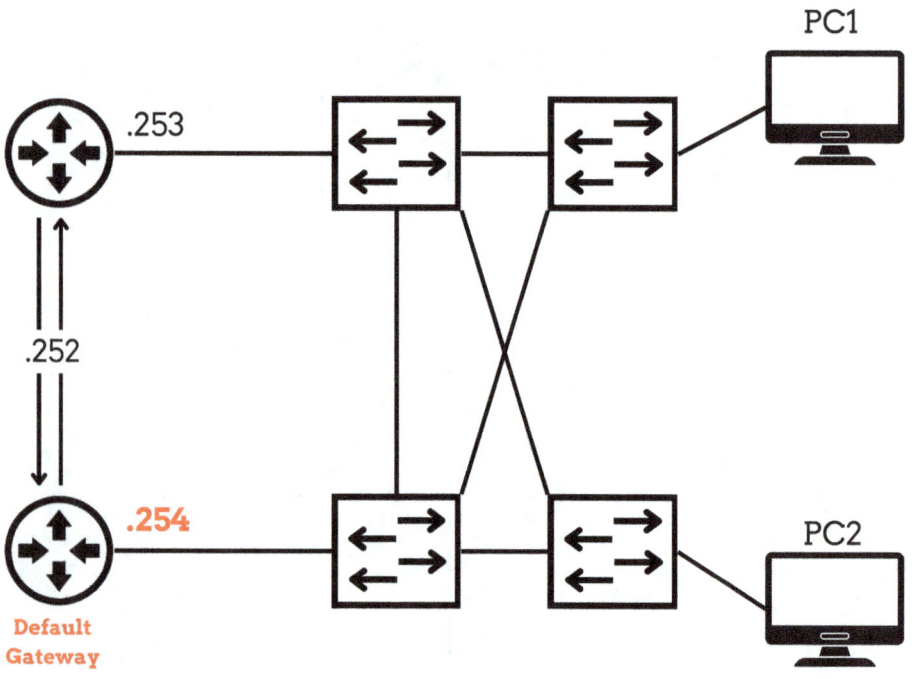

In this example, the default gateway of PC1 and PC2 is .254

But, what if the router .254 shutdown or stops working?

Simply, it will be automatically replaced with the 253 router which is in standby mode, and all this process is done by **FHRP**.

How does FHRP do this?

1- It creates a virtual IP vIP between the two routers which in .252 in the example above.

2- The main router keeps sending "hello" messages to the standby router to indicate that it is still functioning.

3- If the standby router does not receive any hello messages for a while, this means the main router is not working, and the standby router takes over as the main router.

FHRP Summay:

- FHRP ensures a reliable network by providing a backup for the default gateway.
- A virtual IP address (vIP) is shared between multiple routers.
- One router operates as the active router, handling all traffic.
- Another router remains in standby, ready to take over if needed.
- The active router sends "hello" messages to the standby router to indicate it is functioning.
- If the standby router does not receive "hello" messages, it assumes the active router has failed.
- The standby router then becomes the active router, maintaining network traffic flow.

Some FHRP protocols:

- HSRP (Hot Standby Router Protocol): A Cisco proprietary protocol that provides redundancy for IP networks by designating active and standby routers. Only one router is active at a time.

- VRRP (Virtual Router Redundancy Protocol): An open standard protocol similar to HSRP, where one router acts as the master, and others are backups.

- GLBP (Gateway Load Balancing Protocol): A Cisco proprietary protocol that offers redundancy and load balancing by allowing multiple routers to actively share traffic load.

TCP & UDP

TCP

TCP (Transmission Control Protocol): A reliable, connection-oriented protocol used to ensure data is delivered accurately and in order between devices over a network. It establishes a connection, verifies data delivery, and retransmits lost packets if necessary.

TCP Properties:

- TCP is connection-oriented: The hosts communicate to establish a connection before exchanging data.
- TCP provides reliable communication
- TCP provides sequencing: The sequencing allows the destination host to put segments in the correct order even if they arrive out of order
- TCP provides flow control

TCP 3 Way-Handshake

It is the process used to establish a connection between a client and a server in TCP communication. It involves three steps:

1. <u>SYN (Synchronize):</u> The client sends a SYN packet to the server to initiate the connection.
2. <u>SYN-ACK (Synchronize-Acknowledge):</u> The server responds with a SYN-ACK packet to acknowledge the client's request.
3. <u>ACK (Acknowledge):</u> The client sends an ACK packet to confirm the connection is established.

SYN flag
⟶

SYN-ACK flag
⟵

ACK flag
⟶

TCP 4 Way-Handshake

It is the process used to end a connection between a client and a server in TCP communication. It involves four steps:

1. **FIN (Finish):** The sender (client or server) sends a FIN packet to indicate it wants to terminate the connection.
2. **ACK (Acknowledge):** The receiver acknowledges the FIN by sending an ACK packet back.
3. **FIN (Finish):** The receiver sends its own FIN packet to indicate that it also wants to close the connection.
4. **ACK (Acknowledge):** The sender acknowledges the receiver's FIN with an ACK packet, completing the connection termination.

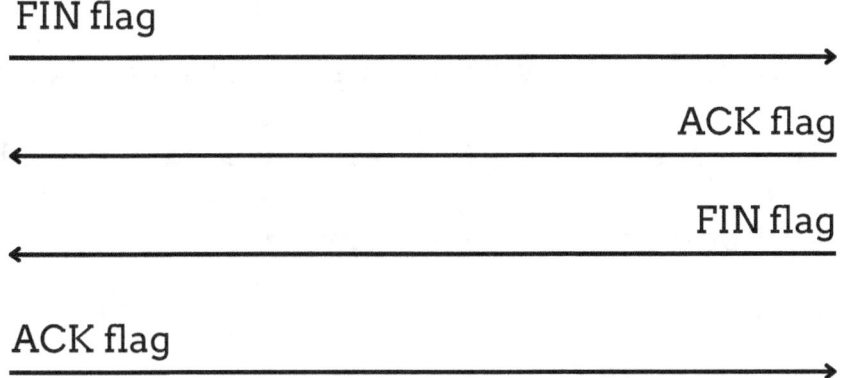

UDP

UDP (User Datagram Protocol): UDP (User Datagram Protocol) is a connectionless and lightweight transport layer protocol used in networking. It allows data to be sent between devices without establishing a connection or performing error checking. This means that UDP is faster but less reliable than TCP.

UDP Properties:

- UDP is not connection-oriented: There is no established connection (3 way-handshake) before sending the data
- UDP does not provide reliable communication, if a segment is lost, UDP has no mechanism to resend it
- UDP does not provide sequencing.

TCP VS UDP

TCP	UDP
Connection-Oriented	Connectionless
Reliable	Unreliable
Supports Sequencing	No Sequencing
Flow control	No Flow control
Used for downloads, file sharing ... etc	Used for VoIP, Live Streaming ... etc

ately been disturbed by protest marches
IPv6

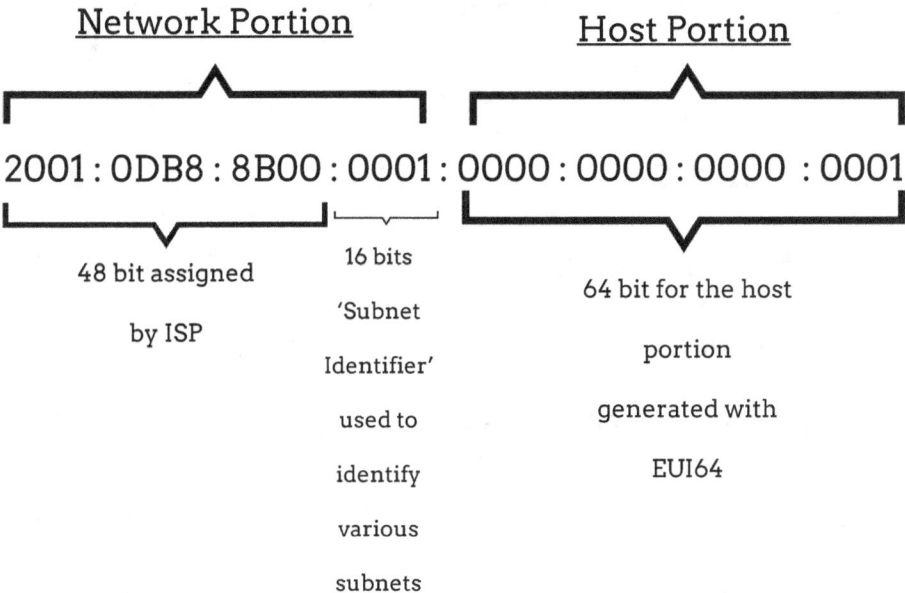

EUI-64:

- EUI-64 is a method of converting a MAC address into a 64 bit interface identifier

- This interface identifier can then become the 'host portion' of a /64 IPv6 address.

How to convert a MAC to an IPv6?

- Split the MAC address: A MAC address is 48 bits long, and you need to split it in half. For example, if the MAC address is 00:14:22:01:23:45, split it into two parts -First half: 00:14:22 -Second half: 01:23:45
- Insert FFFE in the middle: Insert FFFE between the two halves of the MAC address. Now it looks like this: 00:14:22:FF:FE:01:23:45
- Modify the 7th bit: The 7th bit of the first byte of the MAC address needs to be flipped. In the example, the first byte is 00, which in binary is 00000000. Flip the 7th bit (the second leftmost bit). This gives you 02, which in binary is 00000010.
- Final result: After flipping the 7th bit, the address becomes: **02:14:22:FF:FE:01:23:45**

IPv6 Types

- <u>Global Unicast Address (GUA):</u> Routable on the global Internet, similar to public IPv4 addresses.
- <u>Unique Local Address (ULA):</u> Used for local communication within a site or organization. Not routable on the global Internet.
- <u>Link-Local Address:</u> Used for communication within a single network segment or link. Cannot be routed beyond the local network.
- <u>Multicast Address:</u> Used for one-to-many communication, allowing a single sender to send data to multiple receivers.
- <u>Anycast Address:</u> Assigned to multiple interfaces, with data sent to the nearest interface based on routing. There's no specific prefix for anycast in IPv6; any unicast address can be used as an anycast.
- <u>Unicast</u>: One-to-One communication

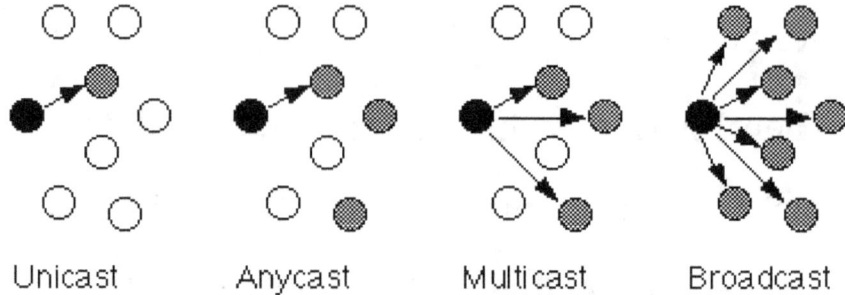

Unicast   Anycast   Multicast   Broadcast

IPv6 Header

4 bits Version	4 bits Priority	24 bits Flow Label	
16 bits Payload Length		8 bits Next Header	8 bits Hop Limit
128 bits Source Address			
128 bits Destination Address			

- **Version**: Indicates the IP version (IPv6 is always 6).
- **Traffic Class:** Used to prioritize packets for better quality of service (QoS).
- **Flow Label:** Identifies packets belonging to the same flow for special handling.
- **Payload Length:** Specifies the length of the data portion (excluding the header).

- **Next Header:** Specifies the type of the next protocol or extension header.
- **Hop Limit:** Limits the number of hops (routers) the packet can pass through.
- **Source Address:** The IPv6 address of the packet's sender.
- **Destination Address:** The IPv6 address of the packet's recipient.

IPv6 Summary

IPv6 is the latest version of the Internet Protocol, using 128-bit addresses to provide a much larger address space than IPv4. It supports three main address types: Global Unicast (public), Link-Local (local network), and Unique Local (private). IPv6 eliminates broadcasts, uses multicast for communication, and has improved security features with mandatory IPsec. It also supports automatic address configuration and is designed for more efficient routing.

ACLs

An **ACL (Access Control List)** is a set of rules used to control traffic on a network. It defines which users or devices can access certain network resources and what kind of actions they can perform (like allow or deny specific traffic). ACLs help manage security by filtering traffic based on IP addresses, protocols, or ports. There are two types of ACLs: Standard ACL and Extended ACL.

STANDARD ACL

1- Filters based on source IP address:
- A Standard ACL only examines the source IP address of the packet.
- It cannot filter traffic based on the destination IP, protocol, or port numbers (like an extended ACL).

2- Range of ACL numbers:
- Standard ACLs are assigned numbers from 1 to 99 (or from 1300 to 1999 for extended ranges in newer devices).
- For example, ACL 1 can be used to configure a basic ACL rule that filters based on source IP addresses.

3-Configuration and Placement:

- Standard ACLs are typically placed as close to the destination as possible (on the router or device receiving the traffic).
- This ensures that traffic is filtered based on source IP addresses before it reaches the internal network.

4-Default Behavior (Implicit Deny):

- If no specific permit or deny rule matches a packet, the default action is to deny the packet. This is called implicit deny and applies to all traffic not explicitly allowed by the ACL.

5-Where to Apply Standard ACLs:

- Standard ACLs are typically applied to the incoming or outgoing traffic on interfaces where filtering is required.

6-When to Use Standard ACLs:

- Simple filtering: When you only need to block or allow traffic based only on the source IP address.
- Network access control: To limit access to certain subnets or networks based on their IP address.

7-Avantages:

- Simpler and easier to configure compared to extended ACLs.
- Good for scenarios where only source IP filtering is required.

8-Disadvantages:

- Limited flexibility: Standard ACLs cannot filter based on destination IP, protocols, or ports. For more complex filtering, extended ACLs are needed.

Example of a standard ACL

ACL 1:

1- if source ip=192.168.1.0/24, then permit

2- if source ip=192.168.2.0/24, then deny

3- if source ip=any , then permit

EXTENDED ACL

An Extended Access Control List (ACL) is a type of Access Control List that provides more detailed traffic filtering by evaluating not only the source IP address but also the destination IP address, protocol types (like TCP, UDP, ICMP), and port numbers. This makes extended ACLs more versatile than standard ACLs, as they can filter traffic based on specific application protocols or services.

1. Filters Based on Multiple Criteria:

- Extended ACLs evaluate source IP address, destination IP address, protocol type, and port numbers.

2. Range of ACL Numbers:

- Extended ACLs use numbers between 100 and 199 (or from 2000 to 2699 for extended ranges in newer devices).
- For example, ACL 100 can be used to configure a more complex filtering rule based on source and destination details.

3. More Flexible Configuration:

- Extended ACLs can filter based on source/destination IP addresses and a wide range of protocols (like TCP, UDP, ICMP).
- You can define specific port numbers for protocols like HTTP (port 80), DNS (port 53), etc., providing more control over what traffic is permitted or denied.

4. Default Behavior (Implicit Deny):

- If no rule matches a packet, the traffic is implicitly denied by default. This is called implicit deny and ensures that traffic is blocked unless explicitly permitted by the ACL.

5. When to Use Extended ACLs:

- Application-Level Filtering: To control traffic for specific applications or services (e.g., blocking HTTP, DNS, or allowing only specific types of TCP traffic).
- Security: Extended ACLs are useful when you need to implement fine-grained security measures, such as allowing only specific types of traffic from trusted sources.

6. Advantages of Extended ACLs:

- More Flexibility: Extended ACLs allow for filtering based on more criteria, providing more precise control over traffic.
- Granular Traffic Control: You can filter traffic based on protocols and ports, which is ideal for controlling access to specific applications or services.
- Enhanced Security: By filtering traffic based on both source and destination IPs, protocols, and ports, extended ACLs offer better security management.

7. Disadvantages of Extended ACLs:

- Complex Configuration: Extended ACLs are more complex to configure than standard ACLs, requiring more detailed information for each rule.
- More Resources: Due to their complexity, extended ACLs may require more processing power to evaluate, especially in large networks with high traffic.

DNS

The Domain Name System (DNS) is like the internet's phonebook. Computers don't understand human-friendly domain names (like www.google.com), so DNS translates them into IP addresses (like 192.168.1.1) that computers use to locate and connect to websites or services.

How does DNS work?
- You type a website's name (like www.example.com) in your browser.
- Your computer sends the name to a DNS resolver to find its IP address.
- The resolver checks its cache for the answer. If it doesn't have it, it asks other DNS servers.
- The resolver first asks a root server, which points it to the Top-Level Domain (TLD) server (e.g., for .com).
- The TLD server directs the resolver to the domain's authoritative DNS server.

- The authoritative server provides the IP address of the website.
- The resolver gives the IP address to your computer, and the browser uses it to connect to the website.

Why it's important?

DNS (Domain Name System) is important because:

1-<u>Simplifies Access:</u> It allows people to use human-friendly names (like www.google.com) instead of hard-to-remember IP addresses (like 142.250.190.78).

2-<u>Connects the Internet:</u> It ensures devices on the internet can find and communicate with each other.

3-<u>Enables Scalability:</u> DNS supports a growing number of websites and services without overwhelming users with technical details.

4-<u>Improves Flexibility:</u> Websites can change their hosting IPs without disrupting users, as DNS updates automatically route traffic to the new address.

Important types of DNS records

- A Record (Address Record): Maps a domain name to an IPv4 address.
- AAAA Record: Maps a domain name to an IPv6 address.
- CNAME Record (Canonical Name): Creates an alias for a domain, pointing it to another domain.
- MX Record (Mail Exchange): Specifies the mail server for handling email for a domain.
- TXT Record: Stores text information for verification or configuration, often used for security purposes.
- NS Record (Name Server): Specifies the authoritative name servers for a domain.
- PTR Record (Pointer): Used for reverse DNS lookups, mapping an IP address to a domain name.

Important types of DNS records

- A Record (Address Record): Maps a domain name to an IPv4 address.
- AAAA Record: Maps a domain name to an IPv6 address.
- CNAME Record (Canonical Name): Creates an alias for a domain, pointing it to another domain.
- MX Record (Mail Exchange): Specifies the mail server for handling email for a domain.
- TXT Record: Stores text information for verification or configuration, often used for security purposes.
- NS Record (Name Server): Specifies the authoritative name servers for a domain.
- PTR Record (Pointer): Used for reverse DNS lookups, mapping an IP address to a domain name.

What's the function of DNS records?

DNS records define how a domain's traffic is managed by mapping domain names to IPs, directing email to mail servers, creating aliases, verifying domain ownership, enabling service discovery, supporting reverse lookups, and providing administrative details about the domain.

DHCP

DHCP (Dynamic Host Configuration Protocol) is a network protocol that automatically assigns IP addresses and other network configuration settings (like subnet mask and default gateway) to devices on a network, allowing them to communicate without manual configuration.

DHCP properties:

1-<u>Dynamic IP Address Assignment:</u> DHCP automatically assigns IP addresses to devices (clients) on a network, eliminating the need for manual IP configuration.

2-<u>Lease Time:</u> IP addresses are leased to devices for a specific period. Once the lease expires, the device must renew or release the IP address.

3-<u>Centralized Management:</u> A DHCP server manages the IP address allocation process, centralizing network configuration and making it easier to manage.

4-<u>Automatic Network Configuration:</u> DHCP provides not only an IP address but also other network settings, such as the default gateway, DNS servers, and subnet mask.

5-<u>Efficient IP Address Usage:</u> DHCP minimizes the risk of IP address conflicts and optimizes the use of available IP addresses in a network.

6-<u>Supports Both IPv4 and IPv6:</u> DHCP works for both IPv4 and IPv6 networks, although the protocols differ in their configuration and handling.

How does DHCP serve IP addresses?

The DHCP process is divided into four steps, often remembered by the acronym **D-O-R-A**:

1. **D** - Discover: The client sends a DHCP Discover message to the network to find a DHCP server.
2. **O** - Offer: The DHCP server responds with a DHCP Offer message, providing an available IP address and other network settings.
3. **R** - Request: The client sends a DHCP Request message to the server, requesting the offered IP address.
4. **A** - Acknowledgment (Ack): The DHCP server sends a DHCP Acknowledgment message to the client, confirming the assignment of the IP address and other settings.

Example:

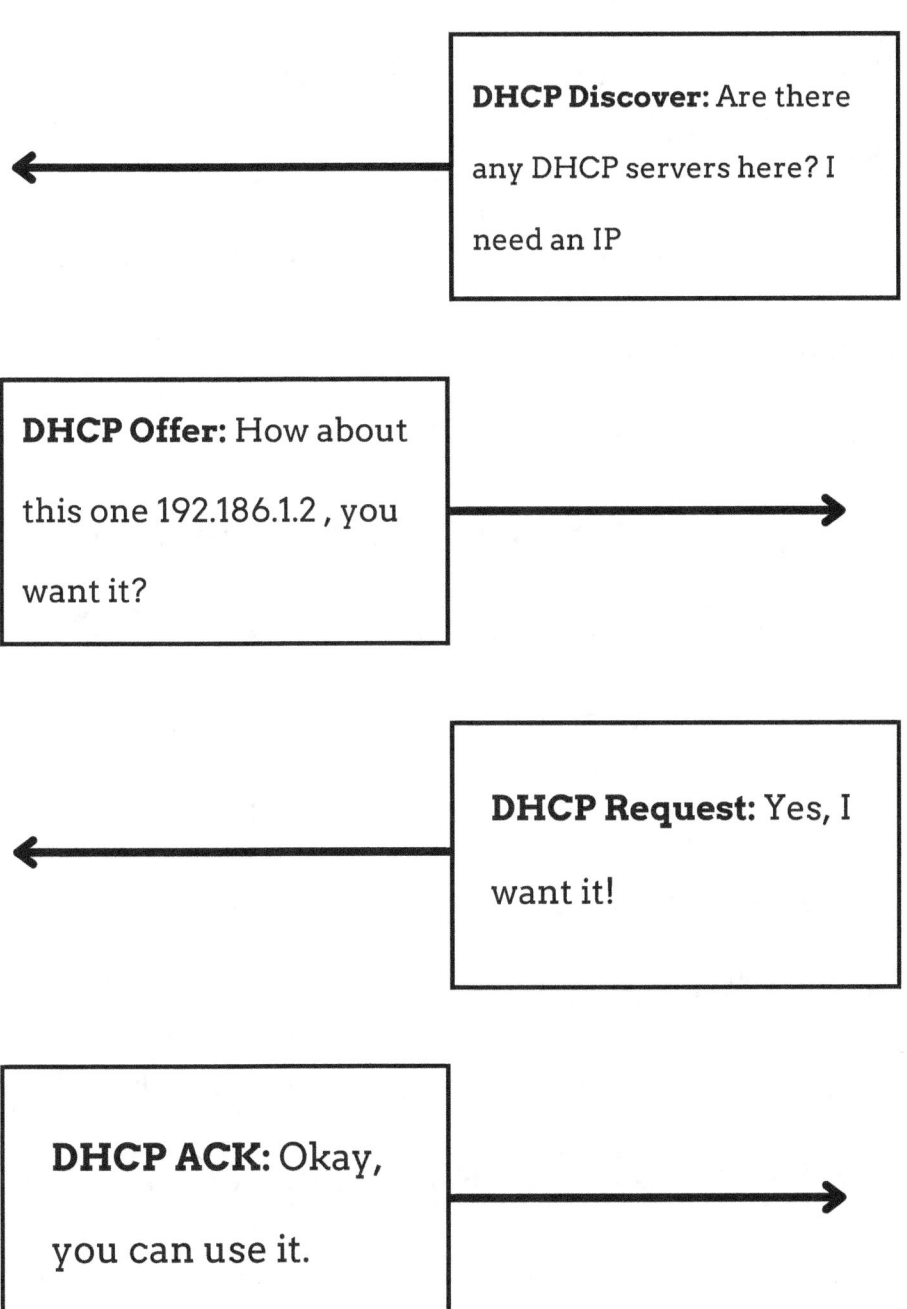

DHCP relay agent

it is a network device or software component that helps forward DHCP messages between clients and servers that are not on the same local network segment.

Here's how it works:

- When a DHCP client is on a different subnet from the DHCP server, the client's DHCP Discover message cannot be directly received by the server because it is broadcasted within the local subnet.

- The DHCP relay agent listens for DHCP Discover messages from clients and then forwards them to the DHCP server on a different subnet.

- The server sends its DHCP Offer back to the relay agent, which then forwards it to the requesting client.
- The process continues for the DHCP Request and DHCP Acknowledgment messages, with the relay agent forwarding messages between the client and server.

Summary:

DHCP is a network protocol that automatically assigns IP addresses and other network configuration information to devices (clients) on a network. It simplifies network management by eliminating the need for manual IP address configuration. The process involves four steps: Discover, Offer, Request, and Acknowledge (DORA).

NAT

PART 1

NAT (Network Address Translation) is a method used by routers to change the IP address of devices in a private network so they can communicate with devices on the internet. It allows many devices in a home or office to share one public IP address, which helps save IP addresses and adds security.

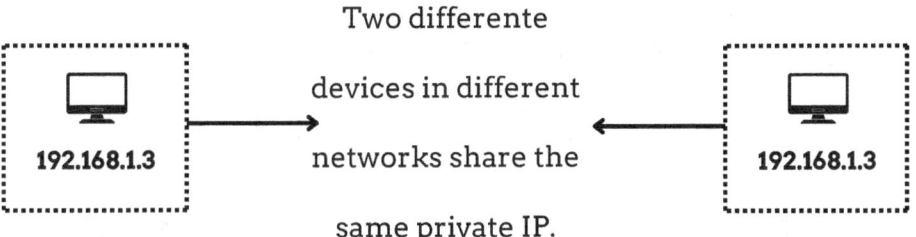

Two differente devices in different networks share the same private IP.

Private IP vs Public IP: What's the difference?

- **Public IP address:** This is the **_unique_** address assigned to a device on the internet. It is routable over the internet and can be accessed from anywhere in the world. Internet Service Providers (ISPs) assign public IP addresses to devices like routers.

- **Private IP address:** This is used within a local network (like your home or office). Private IP addresses are not routable over the internet, meaning they can't be accessed directly from outside the local network. These addresses are used to identify devices within the network, and routers typically use NAT to allow them to communicate with the internet.

Note: Instead of using a private IP, devices use a public IP to access the internet because it's unique, and no two devices can have the same public IP on the internet.

Concept of NAT

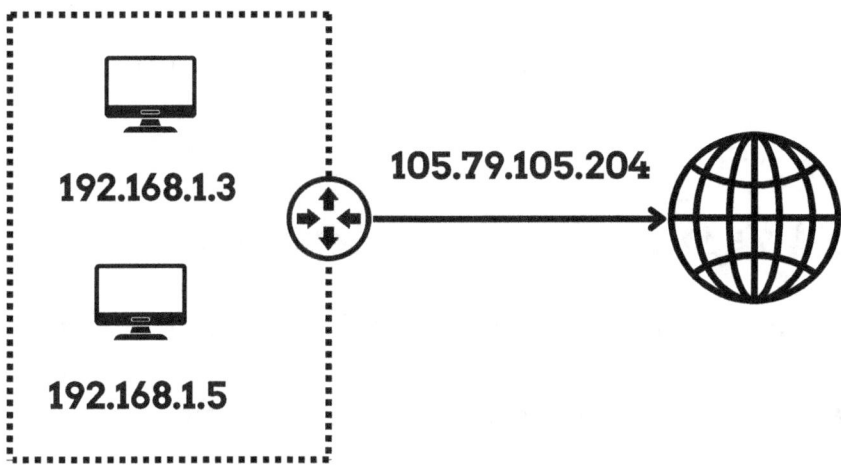

As we can see above, when a PC in the network tries to reach the internet, the router will translate its private IP, which is unique within the local network, to a public IP. As mentioned, each PC has its own private IP (192.168.1.3 and 192.168.1.5), but after the NAT process, all the devices in the network share the same public IP to access the internet. This helps avoid the waste of public IP addresses.

Static NAT

Static NAT (Network Address Translation) is a type of NAT where a one-to-one mapping is created between a private IP address and a public IP address. This means that every time a device with a private IP address accesses the internet, it will use the same public IP address for the translation.

Key Points:

1-Fixed Mapping: The private IP address is permanently mapped to a specific public IP address.

2-Predictable: The mapping remains consistent, so the same public IP will always be used for the same device.

3-Usage: Static NAT is typically used for devices that need to be consistently accessible from outside the network, like web servers or email servers.

Example:

- Private IP: 192.168.1.10   Public IP: 203.0.113.5
- Every time the device with IP 192.168.1.10 communicates with the outside world, it will appear as 203.0.113.5 to the internet.

Advantages:

- Easy to configure for devices that need to be accessed from outside the network.
- Simple and predictable.

Disadvantages:

- Limited scalability: Only a small number of devices can be mapped to public IPs, as it uses a 1:1 relationship.

Dynamic NAT

is a type of NAT where private IP addresses are dynamically mapped to a pool of public IP addresses. Unlike Static NAT, where a fixed mapping exists.

Key Points:

1-Pool of Public IPs: Dynamic NAT uses a group of public IP addresses to map multiple private IP addresses. The router picks an available public IP for translation when a device sends traffic.

2-Temporary Mapping: The mapping is temporary, and once the session ends, the public IP may be returned to the pool.

3-Usage: This type of NAT is commonly used in scenarios where many devices need to access the internet, but there is a limited number of public IP addresses.

Example:

- Private IPs: 192.168.1.10, 192.168.1.11, 192.168.1.12
- Public IP Pool: 203.0.113.5, 203.0.113.6, 203.0.113.7
- If the device 192.168.1.10 makes a request, it might be mapped to 203.0.113.5. The next device, 192.168.1.11, could be mapped to 203.0.113.6, and so on.

We said before that all private IPs have the same public IP, but now we see that each private IP has its public IP, HOW IS THAT? Simply, to avoid configuring static or dynamic NAT each time and assigning a public IP to each device, we just configure **PAT (Port Address Translation)**, so the private IPs share the same public IP with a different port.

QoS

QoS (Quality of Service) is a network management concept that ensures the efficient and reliable delivery of data by prioritizing certain types of traffic. It's used to manage bandwidth, delay, jitter and loss.

1-Bandwidth:

-The overall capacity of the link(bits per second)

-QoS tools allow to reserve a certain amount of link's bndwidth for specific traffic.

example: 20% voice traffice, 30% data traffic, 50% for all other traffic.

2-Delay:

-The amount of time it takes for traffic to go from source to destination and return if necessary.

3-Jitter:

-The small, unpredictable changes in the time it takes for data packets to travel over a network.

4-Loss:

The amount of data packets that fail to reach their destination. This can be caused by issues like faulty cables, network congestion, or when a device's _queues are full_, leading to packet drops.

QoS queuing

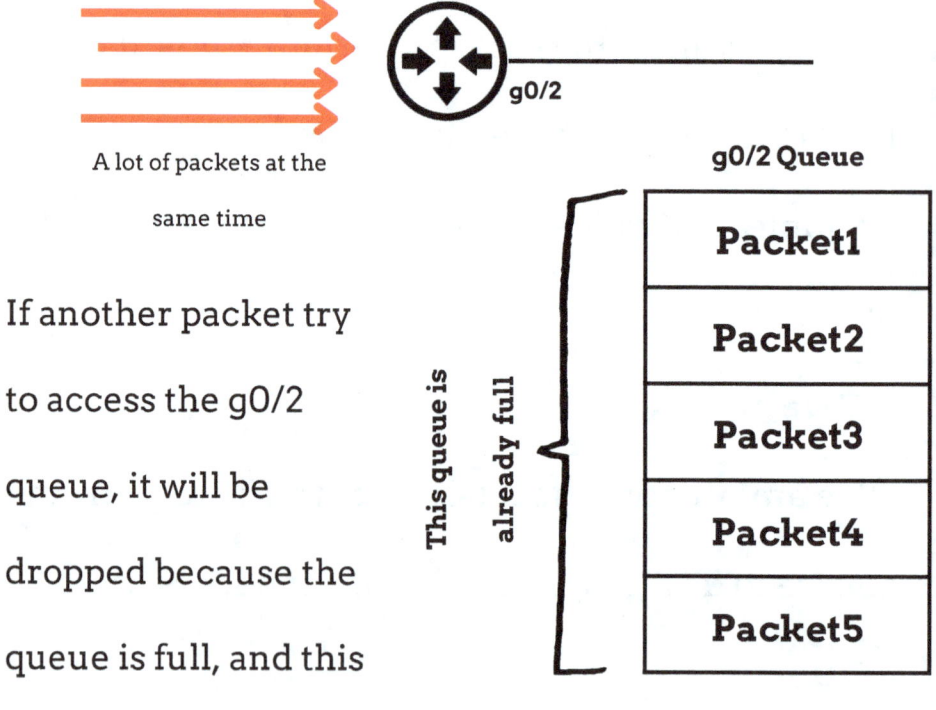

A lot of packets at the same time

g0/2 Queue

If another packet try to access the g0/2 queue, it will be dropped because the queue is full, and this is called **Tail Drop**.

Summary:

Quality of Service (QoS) is a set of techniques used to manage and prioritize network traffic to ensure that critical applications receive the necessary resources for optimal performance. It helps improve the efficiency of a network by controlling bandwidth, reducing delays, minimizing jitter, and preventing packet loss.

LAN & WAN Architectures

LAN

Common Topologies

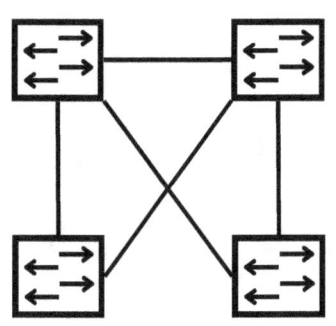

Portal Mesh

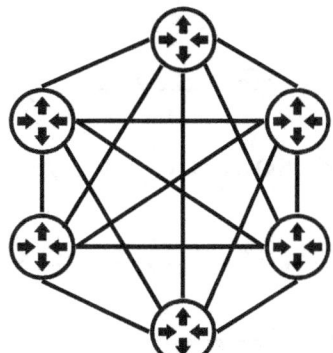

Full Mesh

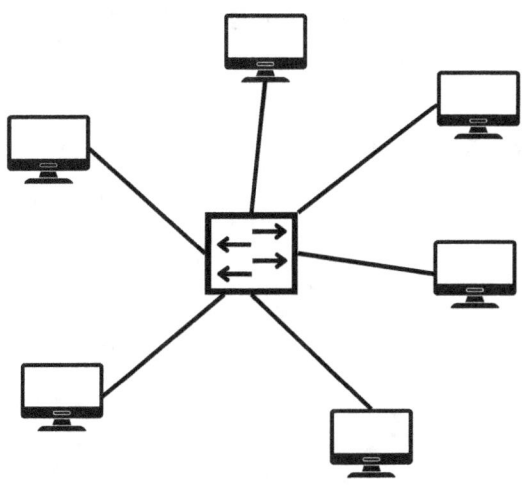

STAR

LAN

2-Tier LAN design

The 2-Tier LAN design consists of 2 layers:

- Access Layer:

-Resonsible of hosts connected to Pc, Printer..etc

-Security services (Port security, DAI...) are done in this layer.

- Distribution Layer:

-Connectes to services such as Internet, WAN... etc

Example of a 2-Tier LAN:

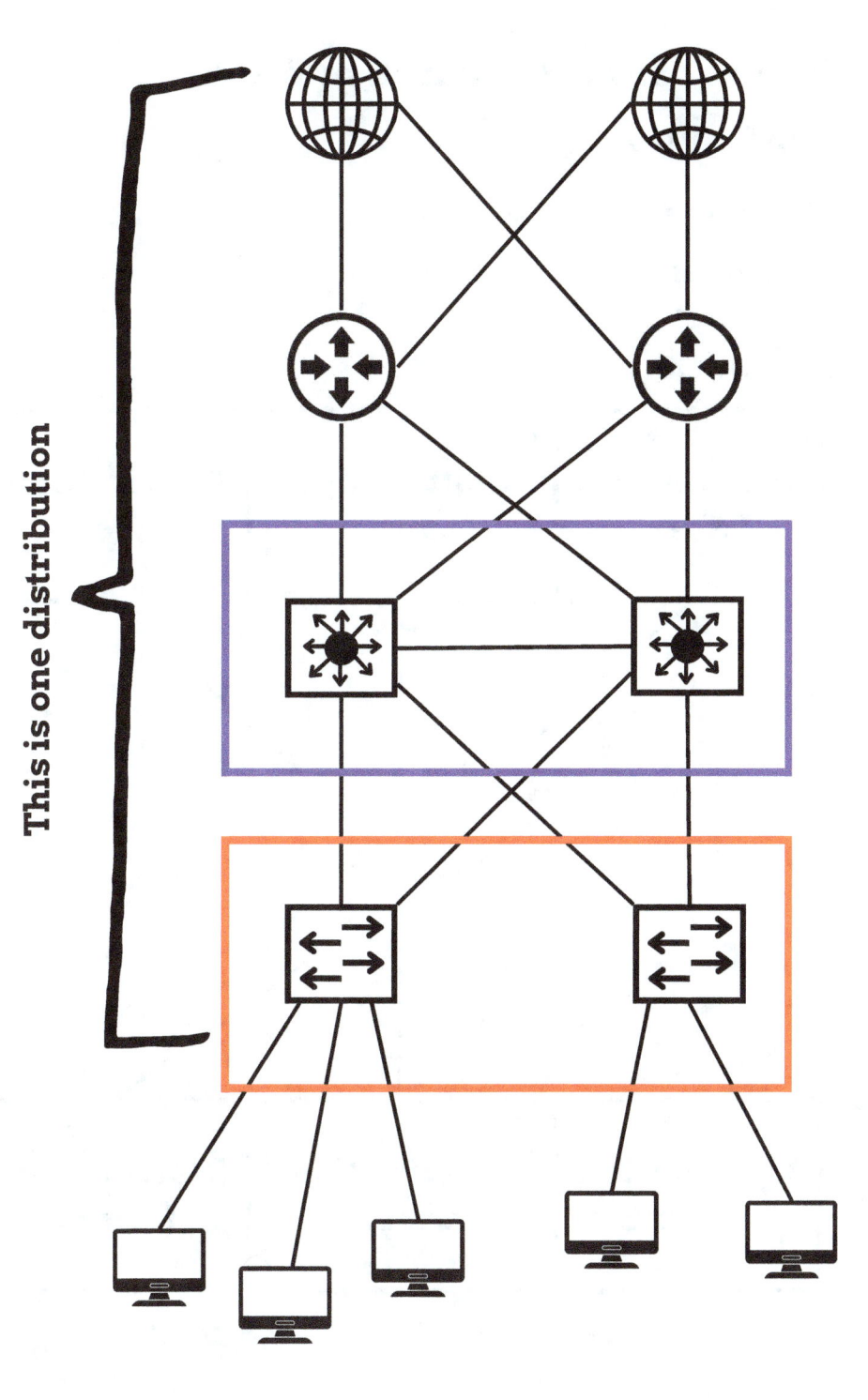

How to connect and link multiple distributions?

-> We insert a core layer

Example:

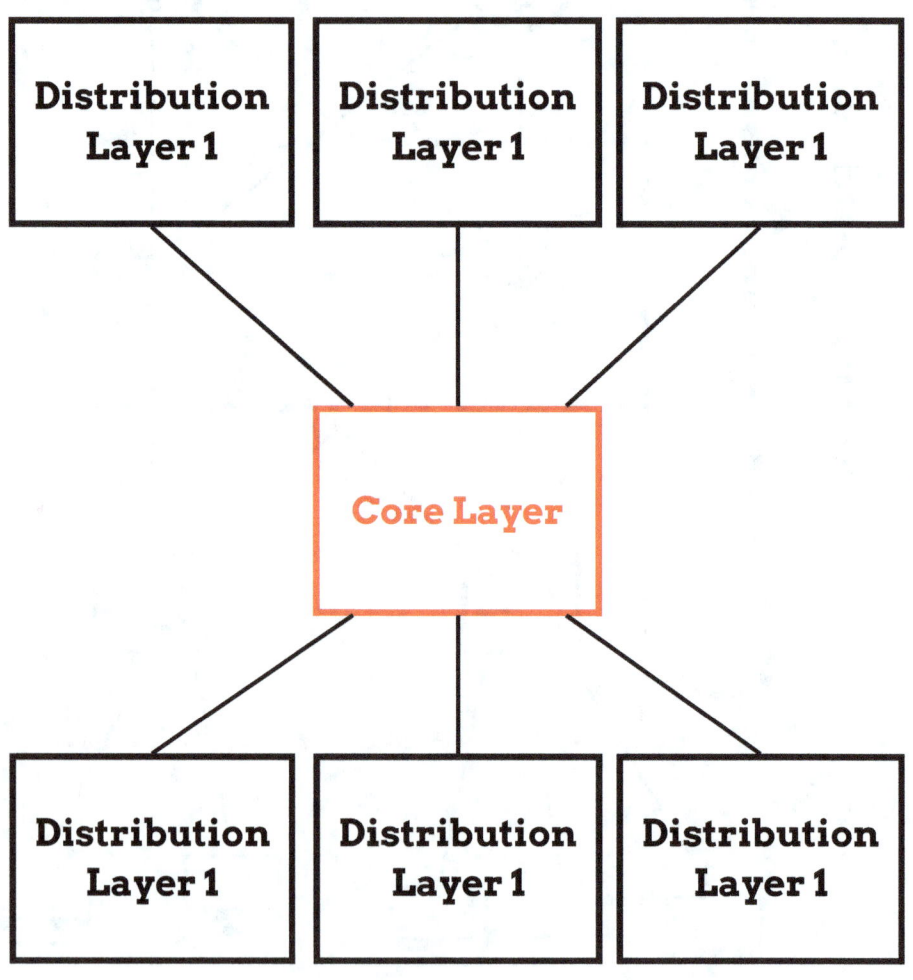

Core Layer:

-A layer to connect and link distribution layers together in a large LAN focusing on speed and fast trasnport of data, and this is the 3 Tier LAN.

2-Tier Vs 3-Tier LAN

Number of Layers:

2-Tier LAN: Consists of two layers—Access and Core. The distribution layer is not present.

3-Tier LAN: Consists of three layers—Access, Distribution, and Core.

Scalability:

2-Tier LAN: Less scalable due to the absence of a dedicated distribution layer, which can lead to bottlenecks as the network grows.

3-Tier LAN: More scalable because the distribution layer handles routing and traffic management, allowing easier growth and better performance.

SOHO networks

Networks like home network that use only the router which can serve as:
- Router
- Switch
- Firewall
- Wireless Accesspoint
- Modem

WAN

-It extends over a large geographic area and connects graphically spearated LANs.

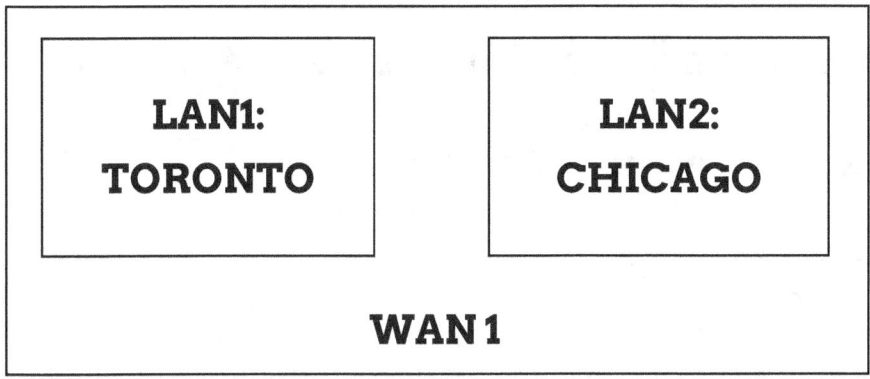

Properties of WAN:

Large Coverage Area:

WAN spans long distances, connecting remote locations.

Uses External Infrastructure:

it relies on services from ISPs or telecom companies (e.g., satellites, fiber optics).

Slower Speeds (Compared to LANs):

Because of the distance, WAN can be slower than local networks.

High Cost:

Setting up and maintaining a WAN is more expensive due to the required infrastructure.

Multiple Technologies:

Uses technologies like MPLS, VPNs, leased lines, and 4G/5G for connectivity.

Centralized Management:

WANs often have centralized control, allowing organizations to manage all branches from a single location.

SPINE-LEAF ARCHITECHTURES

Spine-Leaf Architecture is a modern network design used in data centers. It has two layers:

1. **Spines**: High-speed core switches that connect everything.
2. **Leaves**: Access switches that connect to devices (like servers).

Spine-Leaf properties:

-Every spine switch is connected to every leaf switch.

-Leaf switches do not connect to other leaf switches and same for spine switches

-End hosts connect only to leaf switches.

Example:

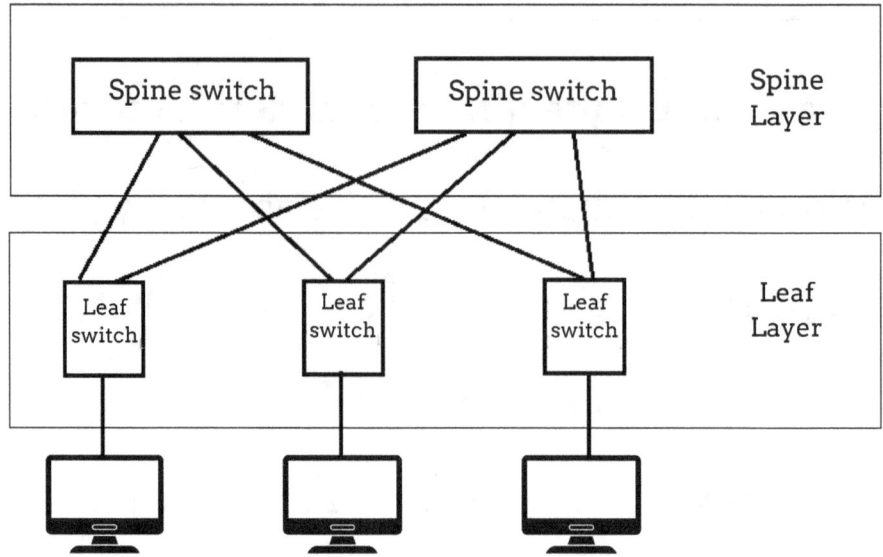

the END.

www.ingramcontent.com/pod-product-compliance
Lightning Source LLC
Chambersburg PA
CBHW071025240526
45469CB00006BD/2098